D1646950

"A Guide to the California Gold Rush"

Front cover:
Wagon train crossing the Great Basin in Nevada
Brompton photo

Dedicated to

Americans & Athena

Past & Present

❦ *A Guide to the California Gold Rush* ❦

Revised Edition

By Eugene R. Hart

Acknowledgments

Special thanks to the California State Library in Sacramento, California

FreeWheel Publications
1173 El Portal Drive
Merced, California 95340-0676
granite@elite.net

All rights reserved,
including the right of reproduction
in whole or in part in any form without special written permission.
Contact FreeWheel Publications to acquire consent to reproduce.
Manufactured in the United States of America
2   3   4   5   6   7   8   9   10

Library of Congress Cataloging-in-Publication Data
Eugene R. Hart
A Guide to the California Gold Rush
p.   cm.
pp. bdg.: 12 pt. cover, 60# alk. paper
Includes bibliographical references and index
1. Gold Rush—United States—California—History—19th century

ISBN 0-9634197-1-2

"Independent publishing for independent thinking."

Copyright © 1993, 2002 by FreeWheel Publications.

❋ Contents ❋

Preface iv

Gold Rush Era Time Line 1

Why Gold, Gold, Gold! 2

Background Summary 4

California Geography 6

The First People of California 9

Who Were the Goldseekers? 12

Transportation to the West 14

To the California Gold Fields 20

Voyage by Sea 21

Journey by Land 27

Where Gold is Found 37

Mining Methods 38

Rise and Fall of the Pony Express 54

The Transcontinental Telegraph 57

Introduction to Towns of the Gold Rush 59

Guide to Towns and Locations 60

Important Dates for California Gold 88

Value of Gold in the 20th Century 90

Glossary of Terms 91

Self-Test Answer Key Directory..93

Bibliography 120

Index 121

✳✳

Preface

The California Gold Rush was an amazing time for anyone to have lived. Even in our modern world we remain curious to share in the dangerous excitement of traversing a half-known continent or vast oceans with the possibility of finding a fortune in California at the journey's end. It was the lottery of the 19th century, and thousands upon thousands were caught up in the intensity of the moment that really wasn't so long ago.

But the Gold Rush era had another side as well. The United States underwent many transitions politically and economically throughout the Western Expansion movement that are even now hard to grasp. During this period the Civil War tested our strength as a nation, and its far-reaching aftermath has shaped the character of this country. There were also rapid progressions in modes of communication and transportation: machine-driven technology we take for granted. In their day, however, they were the equivalent of computer and spacecraft advances. Seldom do we reflect on the inventive developments that have paved important or transparent connections modern society enjoys.

We can't know exactly what it was like to venture across the relatively unmapped western United States in 1849, but we can retrace the timeless route and visualize the arduous journey based on the locations and written records left behind by pioneers who did. Today, one has to look beyond the spellbinding beauty of the land, imposing highways, power lines, fences, and convenience stops when standing next to the places of history. Only then can the dusty faces of hopeful emigrants, sounds of wagons being pulled by sturdy animals, and the earthy smell of trampled sage on a trail long since crossed be imagined. The obstacles and difficulties these travelers of the past dealt with are shut out of our world as we quickly pass once burdensome geography over smoothly paved roads and bridges. The discomfort of desert heat or mountain cold can simply be altered with the turn of a switch as we speed along in automobiles insulating ourselves from the harsh elements that isolate us from their experience.

The reality of a seemingly endless continent to conquer or exploit is gone, and we can see both the good and bad consequences of earlier actions and states of mind. This is where the whirl of history comes into play because we can not change the past, but we can reflect upon it when we attempt to understand our present condition. The people of yesteryear can still be viewed through the evidence of their writings, photographs, objects, and places that opens windows into their time. One such marker of recorded events we can unfold to investigate is the era of the most famous gold rush in the world—California's! Here we may examine the many transformations that have influenced our contemporary world, and in the end maybe we are not as different as we think.

There were two ways to the west coast during the mid 19th century—ship or wagon, but it was the Emigrants' Trail with its many variations that is best known. It was the main artery to the Pacific, and the most widely traveled land emigration route in our history. Departing from the border of western Missouri, the trail connected with the Platte River following it through Nebraska into Wyoming: here it broke off into various cutoffs leading either to Oregon's rich farmlands, or California's gold fields. Diaries, letters, and newspapers of the period describe people, landmarks, and everyday situations along the road that reveal images of adventure, wonder, hardship, and loss. Using a variety of sources, and retracing the trail itself, I researched a modern journey across the western half of the country to the California mining camps. It is my intent to have readers join in exploring the Gold Rush, with reference to some of the incredible surrounding events and changes that in one way or another touches us all.

✳✳

♣ *Gold Rush Era Time Line* ♣

1848   The Mexican War ends resulting in a huge territory, including California, being ceded to the United States. That same year gold is discovered at Sutter's "millseat," in a mountainous river valley known as Coloma.

1849   First wave of approximately 25,000 goldseekers reach California. The safety pin is invented by Walter Hunt.

1850   A second massive migration of roughly 45,000 enters California by land and sea. California becomes the nation's 31st state.

1852   Hydraulic mining originates in California. It will be become widespread throughout the state in the next three decades.

1854   Sacramento is chosen as the state's capital. Gold production hits an all time peak of $69,433,931 (1854 dollars) and declines from this year on. The "Gold Rush" is essentially over except for those who have the money to supply and maintain heavy machinery. Ezra Warner patents the can opener.

1861   The Pony Express comes to an end. The transcontinental telegraph connects the east and west coasts. The Civil War begins.

1865   The War Between the States ends. President Lincoln is assassinated while attending Ford's Theatre in Washington D. C.

1869   The Union and Central Pacific Railroads connect in Utah. This links the Atlantic and Pacific coasts of the United States for the first time by rail.

1876   Alexander Graham Bell publicly demonstrates the telephone. His patent revolutionizes communication.

1879   The electric light bulb is perfected by Thomas Edison and his associates. The technology quickly spreads into public use by the turn of the century.

1884   Hydraulic mining is all but stopped by court order because the waste dumped in rivers causes widespread flooding in the lower valleys.

1898   Dredging is successfully introduced in California. This and hardrock mining continue to profit in the gold region.

1933   Gold reaches a new high of $35 an ounce.

1942   Due to World War II, the government orders all gold mining enterprises that use iron and explosives to halt.

1957   The *Empire and North-Star*, California's most productive underground mines, open since 1850, close for good due to high production expenses.

1968   The last large-scale dredging operation stops due to rising costs and environmental concerns.

1979   Gold reaches an all time high of over $800 an ounce for a short time. This stimulates new exploration and the reopening of some mines.

1985   Modern-day treasure hunters locate the lost Gold Rush era steamship *Central America* off the coast of South Carolina. It contains tons of California gold in various forms that had been sunk in the Atlantic for 128 years.

❖ *Why GOLD, GOLD, GOLD!* ❖

In the world we inhabit, just about anything in short supply is valuable, and gold is one of those things. It could be that rarity is the singular reason we have decided gold is important, but it is truly an amazing element. It does not corrode nor rust and can be shaped into any imaginable creation. In fact, the metal can be pounded so wispy thin, some special candy companies actually cover chocolate with an edible golden wrap: the wrapping is so incredibly fine that 1000 layers would be needed just to match the thickness of one sheet of newspaper! All of us have seen jewelry made from the yellow mineral, and many simply admire the emotional appeal and sparkling gloss of its natural beauty. But gold has played a significant role in the historic past of our energetic republic as well.

The treasure reaped from California during the prime of the rush was vital to the country's progress. Since gold is a common worldwide monetary exchange, the United States Government once stamped coins from the precious metal and used it to back up paper currency guaranteeing its value. Bankers made fortunes buying raw gold from miners in the field for less than top dollar, and later resold it at higher prices sweeping healthy profits. On the other hand, money was made available for personal loans and upstart businesses who created new jobs resulting in widespread economic development and opportunities.

Investors on the east coast who supported expensive mining operations in the Golden State anxiously awaited shipments of heavy gold bars carried by steamships thrashing their way across two oceans. These vessels brought the fruits of California's astonishing riches delivering the means for our evolving nation to expand. Ever growing transportation routes such as railroads that linked the east and west coasts were built with California's hidden wealth. Additionally, major western cities such as Sacramento and San Francisco were constructed with materials purchased with gold. That same gold even provided income for the North during the Civil War. The overall impact of California's glittering bounty, worth over $25 billion today, clearly played a commanding historical role in the advancement of this country. Without California's motivating resource, fewer *emigrants** would have been prompted to move west as quickly, thus affecting the course and expansion of the United States.

It should be remembered, however, that there were Indians living in California long before historically recent explorers came to this land. The first people initially did not fathom the good and bad effects new settlers would have on their way of life, nor could the natives realize that their traditional hunting and gathering grounds would be invaded by droves of goldseekers with ideas, values, **technologies**, and society disconnected from their own. But with news of gold, the trails these first Americans traveled for countless years would be hurriedly crossed and overrun with people from many parts of the world impacting their lives forever.

Nevertheless, this is the way history was written in a long series of events that led to the ultimate western border of present day United States. The purpose of this book is to help you participate in understanding the people, places, conditions and changes that have made this chapter of American history so interesting.

Unidentified Union Civil War soldier from Ohio.

Bold printed words throughout this book are defined in the glossary.

Self-Test: Why GOLD, GOLD, GOLD!

1. List three ways gold is used: _____

_____

_____

_____

_____

2. How is gold important to our society? _____

_____

_____

_____

3. Why do you think gold is valuable? _____

_____

_____

_____

4. Provide at least one example of how California gold helped the growth of the United States:

_____

_____

_____

5. Describe one positive impact you think the goldseekers would have on Native Americans in California: _____

_____

_____

_____

_____

The properties of gold have been valued since the earliest of times. Egyptian and Greek civilizations were using it long before any explorers had reached the western hemisphere. In the Americas, the Incas and Aztecs built rich cultures around the precious metal. And while the natives of early California also knew of its existence, it wasn't a symbol of wealth nor was it important to their culture.

By 1579 the English explorer Sir Francis Drake and his men anchored near San Francisco, what they called the New World, to make repairs on their ship. During their stay contact was made with the local natives, but they possessed no gold. Less than a year later Drake completed his voyage around the world and returned to Europe, but without the knowledge of California's treasure.

The Spanish, who had built a string of 21 missions along the California coast during the 1700s, never knew that less than a hundred miles to the east, in the foothills below the snow-capped mountains they named, lay a fortune. Spanish living in Southern California heard of gold in 1775 while the American Revolution was being fought, but the rumor wasn't enough to cause more than a stir. In 1842 a California Mexican named Francisco Lopez did find gold while working on a large ranch northwest of Los Angeles, but with no far reaching affects. As it so often happens, conditions had to be just right to trigger the events that would unfold into the world's most famous gold rush.

In the spring of 1846 shortly before war broke out between the United States and Mexico, California was taken by a group of overanxious Americans living there. Unhappy with Mexico's neglect of their northern province, and emboldened by the presence of John C. Frémont's small U. S. Government military mapping expedition, they took action. Since the militia was not technically representing the United States, they could not raise the stars and stripes, so a new handmade flag was created. Because of the crudely drawn bear, it became known as the "Bear Flag." Soon Frémont's army joined the premature revolt; a month later war was officially declared by the United States, and within two years it came to a decisive conclusion. California became a territory in 1848, and in that same year gold was discovered by a carpenter named James Marshall who was building a saw mill on the south fork of the American River. This time things would be very, very different.

The timing was right, news spread quickly, and word that easy gold was to be found in California began an excitement unknown to the young republic. Still, people in the east were cautious of the first reports because such far away communications might be unreliable and transportation routes to the west were not well-established. Since few people lived in California, newspaper accounts of

CALIFORNIA REPUBLIC

The original Bear Flag was handmade from white cotton cloth with a four inch red stripe at the bottom. The star and bear were also red and crudely outlined with black ink.

abundant gold might only be rumors. However, in December 1848, the hearsay was finally put to rest when a speech by President James K. Polk, and 230 ounces of gold on display inside the War Department Building in Washington D. C. confirmed the dramatic truth. Thus in the spring of 1849, the largest single migration of people the world has ever known was on! Roughly 25,000 goldseeking hopefuls made the trip to California during the first year of the rush, and in 1850 the Bear Flag Republic became the nation's 31st state.

Self-Test: BACKGROUND SUMMARY

1. Name four early civilizations who used gold before Europeans explored the Americas:

2. Why didn't the Native Americans in California start their own rush for gold?

3. What European explorer made contact with California natives? Why did he stop here? Did he learn anything about gold?

4. How might U. S. history be different if the Spanish had discovered gold first?

5. Who was Francisco Lopez?

6. What was the Bear Flag Revolt?

7. How was gold discovered in 1848 setting the Gold Rush in motion?

8. Why did it take more than a year for the rush to begin?

CALIFORNIA GEOGRAPHY:
MAP "A"

This map shows three general geographical regions in California. Each area is marked with the first letter of its name. Color-code each area with a color of your choice. Throughout this guide the passages you read will refer to the geography you study. Be sure to remember the locations you learn.

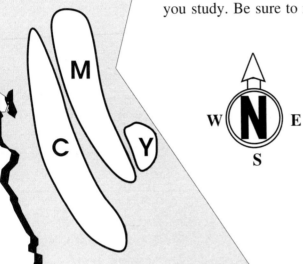

YOSEMITE (Y)

This was one of the last places Native Americans lived untouched in California for hundreds of years. Yosemite is a huge "U" shaped valley carved by ice long ago leaving behind rock walls and waterfalls thousands of feet high. Today, Yosemite is a national park where millions of people come to visit and enjoy its beauty each year.

Color Yosemite

☐ **RED**

The GREAT CENTRAL VALLEY   (C)

This massive, flat valley is made of two major drainage basins: the Sacramento and San Joaquin. The region is known throughout the globe as a famous agricultural center producing a wide variety of crops. This is possible because spring snowmelt from the Sierra Nevada Mountains provides water for **irrigation** during the dry summer growing season. Many nuts, fruits, and vegetables sold across the country and world originate here.

Color the Great Central Valley

☐ **GREEN**

MOTHER LODE   (M)

Although there was no single source of California gold, this term refers to the region where most of it was found during the Gold Rush. The area chiefly sweeps along the foothills of the Sierra Nevada in a northerly-southerly direction. Many trees also cover this area that supplied the fuel and lumber for thousands who came in search of wealth.

Color the Mother Lode

☐ **YELLOW**

Throughout this guide the following geographical landforms will be mentioned so be sure to know their locations for future reference. Use the color-keys to complete this study guide before going to the Self-Test on the next page.

Major RIVERS Where Gold Was Found

TRACE each river on the map of California with a color of your choice as you follow its path.

☐ 1 San Joaquin   ☐ 6 American

☐ 2 Merced   ☐ 7 Bear

☐ 3 Tuolumne   ☐ 8 Yuba

☐ 4 Stanislaus   ☐ 9 Feather

☐ 5 Mokelumne   ☐ 10 Sacramento

Pacific Ocean

10 9 8 7 6 5 4 3 2 1

(10)   (1)

F   T   G

W N E S

LAKE TAHOE (T)

This is the third deepest lake in the world with a depth of over 1600 feet. It formed when two mountain fault lines collapsed creating a basin that filled with water over time. Miners and loggers knew this famous lake well during the 19th century.

☐ **Color Lake Tahoe BLUE**

GOOSE LAKE (G)

This body of water is a natural habitat for wildlife and was a familiar sight to many travelers on Lassen's Cutoff as they rested before continuing to the gold fields.

☐ **Color Goose Lake BROWN**

SAN FRANCISCO BAY (F)

This large, natural bay is California's most famous. The Pacific entrance into the bay is known as the "Golden Gate," and many fortune-hunters sailed through here on their way to the gold fields. Notice that all rivers eventually drain into San Francisco Bay. This made it possible to travel up river from the growing city of San Francisco to jumping-off points within reach of the northern and southern mining districts.

☐ **Color San Francisco Bay area ORANGE**

MOUNTAINS

These prominent natural barriers were well-known to travelers of the day. The Sierra Nevada are steep and rugged on the eastern side to the summit passes, then slope more gradually to the west. The Coast Range, bordering the Pacific Ocean, was not especially hazardous, yet an obstacle to be traversed by those entering or leaving the gold fields by way of California's western shore. With colors of your choice, fill each mountain range symbol on the map.

△ **SIERRA NEVADA**
○ **COAST RANGE**

CALIFORNIA GEOGRAPHY: *Self-Test*

This Self-Test will help you check what you have learned. Identify every feature from memory *before* writing Self-Test answers. Record symbols, letters, and numbers not remembered on the lines in the "restudy" box. If you need to review, examine study guide maps "A" and "B" again.

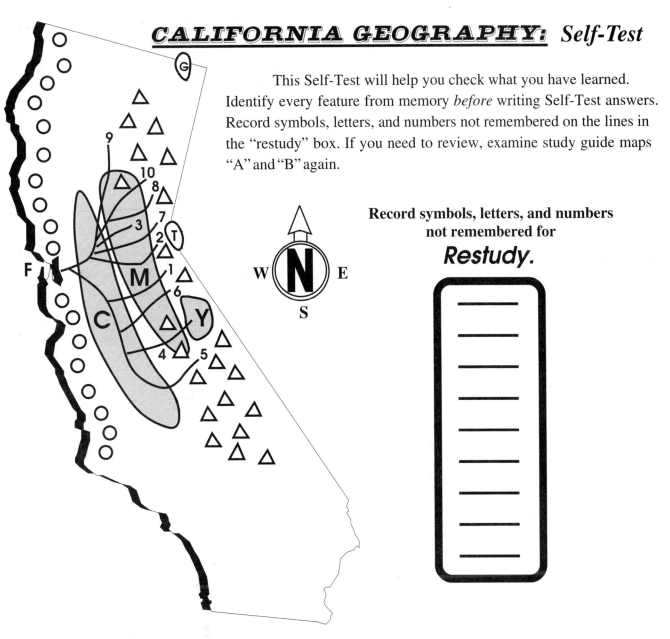

Record symbols, letters, and numbers not remembered for

Restudy.

LABEL THE FOLLOWING GEOGRAPHICAL FEATURES OF CALIFORNIA

(River numbers on Self-Test are different from map "B")

Rivers

1. _____

2. _____

3. _____

4. _____

5. _____

6. _____

7. _____

8. _____

9. _____

10. _____

Mountains

◁ _____

◯ _____

Lakes/Bay

G _____

T _____

F _____

Regions

M _____

Y _____

S _____

The first inhabitants who made North America their home arrived thousands of years ago developing cultures and values independent from the rest of the world. Before explorers came, there were about one hundred different native tribes living throughout California scattered from the Pacific Coast to the eastern side of the Sierra Nevada Mountains. All made use of the natural resources they needed and did little to reshape the land. But what happened to them?

When the Europeans made their permanent appearance in California during the late 1700s, they brought Christianity, disease and the changes brought on by a conquering people. Over the next century this would lead to lasting cultural shifts and the decimation of untold multitudes of natives. By the 1800s only the remoteness of some Sierran tribes kept them protected from outside influences where their cultures remained undisturbed until the invasion of thousands of goldseekers who could not be avoided.

California's original landscapes must have been fantastic sights to behold, and the earliest residents generally treated them with privilege, living in a steady balance with nature and each other. Probably the most beautiful location where the natives gathered is what we now call Yosemite Valley. The Indians named this same canyon "Ah-wah-nee" which can be interpreted as "Deep Grassy Valley,"

and its mixture of various tribes became known as the Ahwahneechee.

Ahwahnee is a breathtaking valley shaped by the powerful forces of glacial ice that melted leaving behind massive rocky cliffs and waterfalls thousands of feet high. With time, this natural hollow of purity cut through by the Merced River eventually supported thick meadows and a variety of plants and animals. This completed the

Yosemite Valley today as seen from Tunnel View.

scenery in an unmatched paradise. Believing their gods had created this special place, Native Americans made this basin their home. Here they fished for trout, hunted deer and small game, and gathered roots. Abundant oak trees supplied the nut meat of acorns providing a main staple of their diet and a reserve of food needed to get them through the winter. The cycle between people and nature prevailed year after year, and the Ahwahneechee had no reason to imagine that it would ever end.

This life-style continued uninterrupted until sometime around 1800 when a disease drove the natives from their unspoiled valley. It was remembered as a "black sickness" and was probably a plague. Many deaths resulted, and the survivors must have reluctantly carried their possessions out of the valley to live among neighboring tribes. The "Deep Grassy Valley" would be uninhabited for a period of time, but its memory was retained through stories told during the long evenings of summer and winter nights.

Almost twenty years passed before a chief of the Miwok tribe named Tenaya returned to Ahwahnee with about two-hundred of his people. For a time things went on as they once had in this lush, green valley of their old home. But by 1850 the foothills were filled with swarms of fortune-hunters bringing their prejudices about Indians and the use of the land as well as unknown technologies. This was a recipe for disaster that caused the two very different cultures to clash.

The gold and new people it attracted made contacts with the natives unavoidable, but all encounters were not necessarily harmful. Some Indians who met miners on friendly terms often traded with the strange looking bearded settlers learning their unfamiliar ways and of the interesting objects they possessed. One newcomer by the name of James Savage set up trading posts and created his own uneasy way of living among the Indians. In order to establish friendly ties, he learned the languages of various tribes and took five wives! Even so, two of his outposts were attacked and destroyed.

The Ahwahneechee resisted the endless intrusion of the unwelcome outsiders who caused rapid change. They participated in killing raids on settlers, then retreated back to the protective rock walls of Ahwahnee that remained mysteriously hidden from the miners. The settlers who made little effort to understand the natives came to know them as "Yosemites" a probable mispronunciation of the word "Uzumaiti" meaning "grizzly bear," a symbol of the Ahwahneechee.

Also adding to the tensions, various tribes took advantage of the opportunity to hunt miners' horses and mules that were easy targets for food. The strain between the cultures worsened as nervous goldseekers who often made no distinction among the different villages and tribes tended to shoot any Indian on sight. This propelled the cycle of terror and revenge. The official government policy was that all Indians who didn't adapt to the newly imposed society were to be either moved to reservations or eliminated, an attitude that was the beginning of the end for these first people.

Encouraged by miners who wanted their lives and claims safeguarded, government officials were soon called in to make peace. Their failure to settle the dispute led to the organization of a small volunteer army the winter of 1851 in the nearby town of Mariposa. Known as the Mariposa Battalion, its members chose James Savage as their leader. He would direct them on a journey up the Merced River into the mountains to carry out the official policy of protecting the interests of the settlers in the southern **Mother Lode** by forcing the Indians onto a reservation.

Within a few days of the Battalion's advance, Savage sent an Indian messenger pressing Tenaya to relocate his people in a peaceful manner. Concluding that he could not stand against the numbers and guns of the angry militia, the chief agreed to lead his people to a Great Central Valley reservation. But in the days that followed, the Battalion was surprised to find out just how few natives were moving toward the arranged camp. Not believing this was the entire tribe, the cautious army was led through deep snow by an Indian guide to the upper rim of the deep valley where they first set eyes on the spectacular hidden canyon of Ahwahnee. As they descended, the secret of Tenaya's natural fortress was revealed, and many of the remaining Ahwahneechee scattered as the intruders penetrated their last stronghold.

In some way all in the Mariposa Battalion must have been impressed by the beauty of the vertical cliffs and waterfalls that had been concealed from them for so long. But as they explored these wonders they also made sure to destroy the Indian's winter food supply. Eventually, the new landlords renamed the canyon. Because most miners called the Ahwahneechee "Yosemites," it was suggested that the valley in which these Native Americans lived in for centuries be named after them. Ahwahnee has been known as Yosemite ever since 1851.

As for Tenaya, he was never able to regroup his people after the invasion and forced removal from his traditional home. He died about a year later while living among the Monos on the eastern side of the Sierra. A way of life had come to an end for these first people of California as it would for many other tribes in the coming years of the Gold Rush.

Self-Test: *The First People of California*

1.   Describe Ahwahnee: _____

_____

_____

_____

2.   Who were the Ahwahneechee and how did they become known as the "Yosemites?"

_____

_____

_____

_____

3.   What caused conflicts between the natives and miners? _____

_____

_____

_____

4.   How did the Mariposa Battalion find the valley of Ahwahnee?

_____

_____

_____

_____

_____

A goldseeker was anyone who decided to pack together the needed supplies and undertake the rigors of travel by land or sea. They were from all walks of life, overwhelmingly male, but after a few months on the trail very few niceties separated the rich and poor, or the educated and illiterate. Tattered clothes and bearded faces eventually became the universal attire of most. The greater part of these enthusiastic adventurers were citizens of the United States, but the Gold Rush attracted people from many other regions around the globe as well. **Ethnic groups** from all over the world were introduced to each others cultures, and beyond the common prejudices of the day, many friendships must have been made with open minds and common goals. This set the tone for the varied community that has always been California.

A majority of goldseekers traveled by land where they quickly realized the burdens of the journey, and upon arrival the small, hard-earned rewards of working the gold fields. Most men expected to make their fortune and return home in a year or two. Very few women came to California at first because it was thought to be a difficult but short-term affair. And while the men were gone, someone had to take care of the children, farms, and businesses. It was women who were quick to fill this demanding role when their men headed west with "gold fever." Unfortunately few ever became rich and had to be content with turning back safely to the comfort of their loved ones, but many decided to make California their permanent home.

By the early 1850s scores of women made the trek to the Golden State. Some came with husbands, others were looking for one; many wanted a new start in life. Countless others came as "ladies of the night." None the worse for wear after their long journey, they were a very welcome sight throughout Mother Lode towns, some of which had a population of 20 or more men for every available female. When women did arrive, they had a civilizing affect on the men. It wasn't long before family homes, churches and schools competed with the saloons and gambling halls that once took up men's idle time. California was changing as a result of the variety of people attracted by the Gold Rush.

Lunch time? Miners working Auburn Ravine with a long tom in 1852. California State Library Archive

Self-Test: WHO WERE THE GOLDSEEKERS?

1. Where did the goldseekers come from? ______________________________

____

____

2. Define ethnic group: ______________________________

____

3. Why wasn't the journey to the gold fields what many expected? ______________

____

____

____

4. What influence did women have when they came west to California? ____________

____

____

5. Imagine you are a young man or woman preparing to set out for California in 1849. Write a short letter explaining your reasons for going west to those you are leaving behind.

Dear ______________________,

____

____

____

____

____

____

____

____

____

____

____

Sincerely, ______________

TRANSPORTATION TO THE WEST

Headway in transportation improvements from 1849 and over the next twenty years was dramatic. Although wagons and ships were the only common forms of travel to the Pacific coast in the middle 1800s, many breakthroughs quickly followed. While thousands of wagons ambled west in the early days of the Gold Rush, they were unable to dependably carry adequate quantities of heavy building materials, machinery, and supplies in the volumes needed for California's ever growing population. Steam and sail ships were prompt to fill this gap as they easily glided into San Francisco's harbor with tons of cargo that could not have been transported any other way. The drawback, however, was that it took months to complete a voyage that committed ships around the hazardous tip of South America.*

By the late 1850s western land routes were well established west of Missouri opening the way for towns. Heavily loaded freight wagons also began making regular but long awaited deliveries to the Pacific coast that competed with sailing vessels. Stagecoaches soon operated along these same roads condensing the typical 2000 mile, 150 day journey of 1849 into less than a month. That in itself was remarkable for the time, but in ten years there would be even more stirring change. 1869 was a national milestone when the United States built its own **transcontinental** railroad that spanned the nation shrinking the time it took to reach California to less than a week—an amazing accomplishment for the day. This progression of advances in transportation no doubt impressed earlier travelers who had originally made the dangerous trip west, as developments continued to make travel easier and safer.

Steam trains once linked passengers and goods across the United States and everywhere in between. F. P. A. Photo

Americans built the first transcontinental railroad across the Isthmus of Panama in 1855. This made it possible to send goods, and travel west much easier than by the longer Cape Horn route. The Panama Canal would not be completed until 1914.

BY WAGON

Transportation by land in the early stages of the Gold Rush was limited to a selection of commonly used boxy wagons with canvas covered tops. They were functional and affordable, requiring minimal modifications to prepare them for the constant abuse a journey to California would demand. There were a variety of styles to choose from, but the most typical were the standard farm wagon and the heavy-duty, German-designed Conestoga.

At a length of 15 to 18 feet, the Conestoga had a wide sweeping body with tall upward slanting ends to keep belongings from sliding out when navigating steep hills. Its rugged construction, huge wheels and high axles made traveling over rocks, tree stumps or washouts considerably easier to pass. But even with those advantages relatively few Conestogas were outfitted for the long trip to the gold fields. Cost, size, and the heavy loads they were capable of handling would be too burdensome for the animals that had to pull them on grueling mountainous trails farther west.

Much more popular was the simple but sturdy standard farm wagons that just about every family owned on the farms of agricultural America. These manageable vehicles were 12 to 14 feet long, about four feet wide and much lighter than the Conestoga. Thousands of these serviceable wagons would roll into California during the Gold Rush and beyond.

All of these "prairie schooners," or ships of the land had some features in common. Each was covered with a protective white canvas top, and some were treated with a tacky waterproofing mixture of beeswax and linseed oil which gave them a sandy brown color. The body was often painted an eye-catching light blue or green with red wheels, but cheerful colors did not disguise the fact that every one had an uncomfortable ride. Because there was no suspension whatsoever, riding a team animal or more often walking was less tiring than a jolting wagon.

It was recommended that no more than 2000 pounds of supplies should be carried on board for the four to six month journey to California; however, many were grossly weighted down beyond this. Each was pulled by an average team of four to six oxen or mules which would haul the necessary supplies for about five travelers on their journey west. With the above specifics in mind, it was generally only the driver, the very tired or sick who rode inside the heavily loaded wagons.

A majority of people used this familiar method of transportation, sailing ships being the only other option, to reach the gold fields in 1849. It was geography that imposed the greatest limitations that extended the amount of time required to span the country. Nevertheless, better roads and technology would quickly shorten the time it took to cross the massive western expanse of the continent.

Scotts Bluff, Nebraska. Wagon "tires" were smaller on front for easier steering.

BY STEAMSHIP

If the geography of traveling across mountains and deserts seemed too frightening, and a person lived near a seaport where experienced captains who sailed the open seas could be relied upon, then transportation by steamship was the alternative. These sturdy work horses of the sea were outfitted with basic passenger comforts, and most were also equipped with sails to take advantage of the wind or head-off the possibility of running out of fuel on a long voyage. But progress was insured during stretches of calm seas or tossing storms with energy created by a coal or wood burning boiler. Steam the engine generated turned large side-mounted paddle wheels that provided dependable power to keep the vessel on course during the long journey across two oceans to California.

These stable wooden ships ranged from 100 to almost 300 feet in length, and were often filled to capacity with hopeful adventurers. The price of a ticket and expenses averaged several hundred dollars for general steerage to twice that much for first class boarding that included ice in drinks. Although voyage by sea could take the same amount of time as traveling by wagon, it was considered safer. The biggest challenge on a steamship was to keep occupied during the long uneventful days on the ocean, or contain pensive thoughts of terror during the occasional foggy or violent weather.

In addition to carrying passengers, these steamships were a vital supply link in the early days of the Gold Rush. Since roads east of the Missouri River were not yet practical for a California supply route, these dutiful ships brought every imaginable commodity to San Francisco such as lumber, bricks, tools, clothes, canned foods, mining equipment, stagecoaches, carriages, train engines, mail, and even the workings for a courthouse clock. Name it, and it was shipped to the west by sea.

More than 25,000 people elected to take the ocean route to California during the first two years of the rush—a minority compared to those who traveled by land, but the return trip was quite different. Not wanting to suffer the hardships of the overland trail again, the vast majority of miners returned by one of the sea routes. Upon leaving San Francisco, they sailed to Mexico, Nicaragua, or Panama where they recrossed a narrower portion of the continent and connected with an eastbound ship to complete the final leg of their journey home. There was no shortage of passengers, and steamships, trailing their long plumes of thick, black smoke, would accommodate all for many years to come.

The SS California delivered the first goldseekers in 1849 and mail for many years thereafter. California State Library Archive

BY STAGECOACH

By 1860 settlements throughout the west had taken hold, and the stagecoach was a common sight making its way across the well-known roads of the plains, mountains, and deserts of the west. Unlike prairie schooners, stagecoaches had suspension systems made of layers of thick leather that ran underneath the coach's wooden body supporting its weight. The ride was elastic, but compared to wagons it was luxury.

If fully loaded, the inside was cramped with nine passengers. There were six facing each other from the front and rear of the coach with three more sitting on the folding seat between the doors. In addition to the two drivers, three more passengers could be seated on the roof. Some luggage and freight went on the roof too, but most of it was mounted on the back of the coach under a leather covering called a "boot" that kept off some of the dust. Unfortunately for the travelers, they usually didn't arrive at their destinations very clean, since a team of four to six horses kicked up a lot of grime in the air.

The cost to ride the stage west was about $300 from St. Joseph to Sacramento and lasted an average three weeks. Relay stops were frequent to harness fresh horses, but after a long day on the road with knees jammed against those of another, it must have been a good feeling to know that there was at least the possibility of a soft bed and a hot meal each evening at the coach's home station. At any rate, the speed of horses was a much faster choice of transportation for traveling the well-established and improved dirt roads across the country.

Typical stagecoach of the mid-nineteenth century.

BY RAILROAD

Railroads had been operating in the United States since the 1830s, and the need to build a transcontinental railway connecting the east and west coasts was recognized as early as the 1850s. But the amount of money, materials and men needed to accomplish such a project was almost unthinkable. Some thought the venture would take thirty years to complete since the granite rock of the Sierra Nevada would have to be chiseled through on the Pacific side. While at the same time, workers from the east laying track on the relatively flat prairie would face possible attacks by hostile Plains Indians.

Despite numerous problems, with the end of the Civil War in 1865, construction of a transcontinental railroad began to take shape. Final plans were drawn for this monumental task as two groups of workers were organized to lay tracks from opposite ends of the country. One outfit, the Central Pacific starting out from Sacramento, hired thousands of laborers including many Chinese who picked and blasted their way through the rugged mountains of the Sierra. The other group, the Union Pacific, hired many ex-Civil War soldiers and Irish immigrants who began to lay track a year later across the plains beginning from Omaha, Nebraska. Working at full speed, men on both teams labored exhausting weeks earning $2 to $4 a day, good wages for the time, while living in mobile tent camps to complete the job at hand.

On May 10, 1869 in less than four years, the two crews met for a celebration at a desolate place named Promontory Summit on the north side of Utah's Great Salt Lake. In all, the Central Pacific laid 742 miles of track and the Union Pacific 1038. In the golden spike dedication ceremony that followed, two engines, one coming from the east and the other from the west, clanked noses as telegraph operators and photographers marked the successful meeting of this impressive achievement. The Atlantic coast was suddenly a week away from the Pacific! In less than twenty years, a long, difficult, and sometimes deadly course that once took six months of travel was now safely measured in days.

Route of the Transcontinental Railroad

"Jupiter"   "No. 119"

Promontory Summit

Omaha, Nebraska

Great Salt Lake, Utah

Sacramento, California

Meeting at Promontory Summit, Utah

Promontory Summit Ceremony. Courtesy Union Pacific Railroad, Omaha, Nebraska

The first engines to run on these tracks were noisy machines whose steam boilers were fed chunks of wood or coal that belched out black smoke and water vapor through their funnels as they puffed along. At an average speed of twenty miles an hour, an engine pulled a series of wooden coaches equipped with beds, lighted by kerosene lamps and heated with potbellied stoves. General passengers paid $75 for a journey that left Omaha, made nearly two-hundred stops to pick up or drop off ticket holders, top off the boiler's water tank or fuel bin, and arrived in Sacramento five days later. Troublesome as it may seem to us, railroads served their purpose: bridging the nation, connecting people, and delivering goods with great speed, comfort and safety for the day. It wouldn't be many years before automobiles, then aircraft made the next major breakthroughs in transportation whisking us along ever faster.

Self-Test: TRANSPORTATION TO THE WEST

Write a short description for each of the following methods of transportation. Include at least one advantage or disadvantage of each:

CONESTOGA WAGON

STANDARD WAGON

STEAMSHIP

STAGECOACH

RAILROAD

⚓ TO THE CALIFORNIA GOLD FIELDS ⚓

The fresh smell of crushed grass and wet earth filled the cool morning air with excitement as hundreds of rattling wagons etched ruts into the rolling green vastness of the prairie. An endless backdrop of cloud-drift blue sky highlighted the drama of the day in the spring of 1849 as mules and oxen bellowed out to their drivers, who were in turn shouting a variety of commands encouraging their teams to pull the heavily loaded rigs.

A wagon stuck to the axle in a muddy bog from a rainstorm the night before was hardly noticed as company leaders rerouted their lineups on both sides of the trail creating new ones. A dog chased a small rodent between a wagon's iron-hooped wooden wheels, as a young woman walking with a friend commented that the eternal lines of wagons resembled chains of ships on a sea of waving grass mixed with splashing multicolored wildflowers.

Another emigrant on a horse, fearful of the unknown, was checking the grease-packed barrels of the new ball and cap revolver he had recently purchased. The sweet smoke of thickly cut fried bacon from a late starter drifted in the breeze. While each day blended in with the next, so continued the epic journey of the goldseeking adventurers who became known by the year they traveled west—'49ers.

Draw your own scene from the passage above as the wagons rolled west across the prairie.

By early August 1848, news of gold on the American River had reached eastern cities in all thirty states. But more convincing evidence would need to be presented to the public in order to overcome doubts of rumors, the expense, and danger of an extended journey to the far west. The long awaited facts were finally confirmed by two unquestionable sources: the United States Army and the President.

The military still occupied California after the War with Mexico, and during this time had witnessed firsthand accounts of gold strikes. This information was forwarded to their Commander-in-Chief along with tangible samples of the valuable metal to backup their reports. Therefore, President Polk could speak confidently with a single, yet powerful sentence during his State of the Union Address to Congress, and the nation December 5th:

> *"The accounts of the abundance of gold in that territory*
> *are of such extraordinary character as*
> *would scarcely command belief were they not [supported]*
> *by authentic reports of officers in public service."*

With those fateful words and 230 ounces of gold on public display at the War Department Building in Washington, D.C., events began to take shape. Seemingly at once, every type of person ranging from farmers to city dwellers, preachers to businessmen, the honest to the swindler, all gathered their savings or sold everything they owned and set out to find their fortune. But first a choice of transportation had to be made. . . to go by land or sea?*

The clipper ship Flying Cloud loading at a wharf in New York. California State Library Archive

* Preview Voyage by Sea Map page 26 to become familiar with the locations you will be reading about before continuing.

If a goldseeker lived inland the decision was simple for most; he would take the land route. He probably already owned a wagon, animals, or had ready cash, and was knowledgeable with the ways of the land. On the other hand, for those living closer to the Atlantic seaboard, the ocean route was a practical way to the gold fields, and getting there as quickly as possible was a consideration. Secondly, ships were available for transportation by east coast merchants and fishermen who sailed around South America's Cape Horn: these captains had earned seaworthy reputations having previously navigated the 17,000 mile voyage to San Francisco. And by the standards of the day, expenses for ocean passage totaled about $400 which cost no more than those preparing to travel by land. It was generally considered safer too. Unlike the overland route, where difficult trails, or failing to find water or grass for the animals could end in disaster, ships were prepared for just about anything except the rarity of a collision or hurricane. These facts made voyage by sea a comforting preference for thousands of anxious goldseekers.

There were other advantages in choosing an oceangoing vessel over a wagon train as well. It was less taxing on the body, and could additionally be much, much faster. Two main sea routes led to California: Cape Horn and Panama. By choosing the shortest route through Panama, an **argonaut** could board a stateside ship and travel by way of Havana, Cuba enroute to Chagres, Panama. There he would leave the Atlantic side, and traverse the **Isthmus** by river canoe and pack mules through a dense jungle trail. He would reach Panama City on the Pacific side in about three days where a northbound ship would speed him to his destination—San Francisco—total time—about six weeks.

Unfortunately in 1849, the rainy passage across the Isthmus had its problems with tropical

The SS George Law, 272 feet long.   Courtesy of the Mariner's Museum, Newport News, Virginia

This same steamship was renamed the Central America *after years of service and over 40 voyages to its credit. The ship transported passengers, mail and shipments of California gold that crossed the Isthmus of Panama enroute to New York. It met with disaster in the year 1857 on Saturday September 12 just after 8 PM sinking in a hurricane off the coast of South Carolina. Hundreds of lives were lost and tons of gold went down with the ship in deep Atlantic water. The gold was recovered in the 1990s by the Columbus-America Discovery Group.*

diseases such as **malaria**. Also, there was a lack of regularly scheduled ships arriving in port on the western side of Panama: a potentially unhealthy and unforeseen delay that could make this endeavor last more than twice its predicted duration. In brief, the only way a traveler could guarantee his surest way to California in the first two years of the rush was by taking the long route around the southern tip or "Horn" of South America on a supply ship. These passengers would endure a voyage that lasted anywhere from four to as many as six months, depending on varying circumstances.

Three major U. S. harbors on the east and south coasts that departed with argonauts for the Cape Horn Route were in New York, Boston and New Orleans. A trip around the Horn that began in mid-January would easily put a voyager in the California gold diggings no later than May or June. There were two kinds of ships readied for the long passage: steam and sail. One style of sailing ship, known as a clipper, had a streamlined hull and was propelled by a massive arrangement of wind sails. The other choice, steamship, could also be driven by the wind, but its source of power was insured with the authority of a boiler that rotated water-churning paddle wheels if the winds ceased to blow.

When a captain gave the order to pull anchor, say from New York, he could take advantage of the Atlantic tradewinds that would help guide his ship and crowded deck of passengers beyond the eastern edge of South America. Making their way into the balmy temperatures below the equator, the next stop would be the city of Rio de Janeiro where they would arrive sometime in February. After resupplying the ship, passengers sailed once again with hopeful expectations. As the voyagers made their way into the southern latitudes, however, the temperature became cooler, and more rain, tossing seas and blinding fog prevailed. It was at this point the easterly winds could become less predictable, and steam power would be an advantage to stay the course.

Although sometimes sailing within sight of the coast, it would be many days before the travelers set foot on land again. During this time argonauts mostly dealt with long periods of boredom, but occasionally they were forced to consider the possibility that swirling fog might conceal hidden obstructions they could strike, or a fearful storm tear apart their ship. As they steamed along, the frigid days deep in the southern hemisphere caused the goldseekers to stay inside the holds of their ship. Many huddled around potbellied stoves passing their time by telling or listening to stories, perhaps while eating a bland meal of hard bread, molasses and pickled beef. The dullness of the trip was frequently broken up by reading, keeping a diary, playing music and singing, card and board games, fishing, shooting empty bottles thrown into the water, watching a fight brought on by worn nerves and confined conditions, or witnessing an unfortunate who couldn't keep his food down because of seasickness; but seldom did the daily routine change.

The passing of the Falkland Islands during March signaled the next part of the journey. The waters of the South Atlantic were often rough, and the dangerous rocky currents of the Strait of Magellan were generally avoided in favor of a more southerly rounding of the continent's tip—Cape Horn. In choosing the safer route, the hazardous strait was bypassed leaving behind the ghosts of countless shipwrecks where less fortunate adventurers over the centuries lay forgotten in deep, icy, grey water.

After rounding the Horn, about two weeks slipped away on the Pacific before they anchored in the port of Valparaiso, Chili. Here, solid land could once again be walked on while the steamship's fuel bin was refilled, and much needed supplies such as fresh meat, vegetables and water were obtained. Taking a few days rest, the voyage continued toward harbors in Callao, Peru or Panama City for one last resupply before reaching their final destination.

By April, hot, sunny weather and calm, favorable seas had replaced the stormy cold as they sailed on a northwesterly course toward Panama. A ship's arrival in Panama City was a big event for waiting argonauts who crossed the Isthmus, as many were now assured passage to California. Farther north, portages might also be made at San Juan, Nicaragua, or Acapulco, Mexico, but they were usually only visited if there was mail to deliver or room to pick up more passengers. On the return trip, however, they were major stops and points of departure for those returning to the states by land across Mexico east to Veracruz, or to the Atlantic side of Nicaragua enroute to San Juan (North). But for now another twenty days would elapse upon leaving Panama when the captain set his final course for California.

In anticipation of steaming into San Francisco Bay, passengers and crew alike crowded the ship's deck to celebrate the end of their long voyage as they passed through the foggy entrance of California's *Golden Gate. It wasn't long before open patches in the thinning mist revealed the ever-growing city of San Francisco—and just beyond, the first hints of the land that held their desires and dreams. As their vessel safely anchored, the appearance of countless ships became visible with masts sticking up high in the air like giant toothpicks on end; they filled every gap of San Francisco's harbor. Once on shore, excited passengers frantically sought needed supplies and made arrangements to pass through the Coast Range to the northern or southern mining districts. This was achieved by sailing up the Sacramento River to Sacramento City or Marysville, or by taking the San Joaquin River to Stockton. From any of those cities the gold fields on the western slope of the Sierra could be reached by crossing the Great Central Valley by wagon, animal or on foot.

**While in port, some captains found themselves deserted by their crews who caught gold fever and left with the passengers! Since construction could not keep up with the demands of this ever expanding city, the stranded captains became businessmen of a sort by selling sections of their worn sails for tents or renting their ships as warehouses, saloons, jails and hotels. In one case a ship was converted to a church. These captains were quick to take advantage of this profitable market. Businesses of all kinds were booming in the once sleepy port of San Francisco, and it wasn't long before merchants who supplied the miners realized that they had discovered the *real* gold mines.

View of San Francisco, California 1850. By the peak of the rush, approximately 700 ships filled San Francisco's harbor.
California State Library Archive

* The term Golden Gate was first used by John C. Frémont in 1846 and refers to the narrow entrance into San Francisco Bay.

**A fun book to read about travel by sea to the Gold Rush is By the Great Horn Spoon authored by Sid Fleischman. The book is fictional, but is based on many facts of the time.

24

1. Why didn't early newspaper reports convince most people in the eastern states there was really gold in California?_____

_____

_____

2. What two things led people to believe there truly was a gold rush?_____

_____

3. What were two advantages of the sea route compared to traveling by land? _____

_____

_____

4. Why wasn't the route through Panama always the best choice in 1849? _____

_____

_____

5. Why did many travelers choose the longer route around Cape Horn? _____

_____

_____

6. What were some of the problems aboard ship during the voyage?_____

_____

_____

7. How did some captains deal with their situations when their crews abandoned ship in San Francisco?_____

_____

_____

8. What do you think is meant by: *Merchants were the ones who discovered the real gold mines.*

_____

_____

MAPACTIVITY: *VOYAGE BY SEA TO CALIFORNIA*

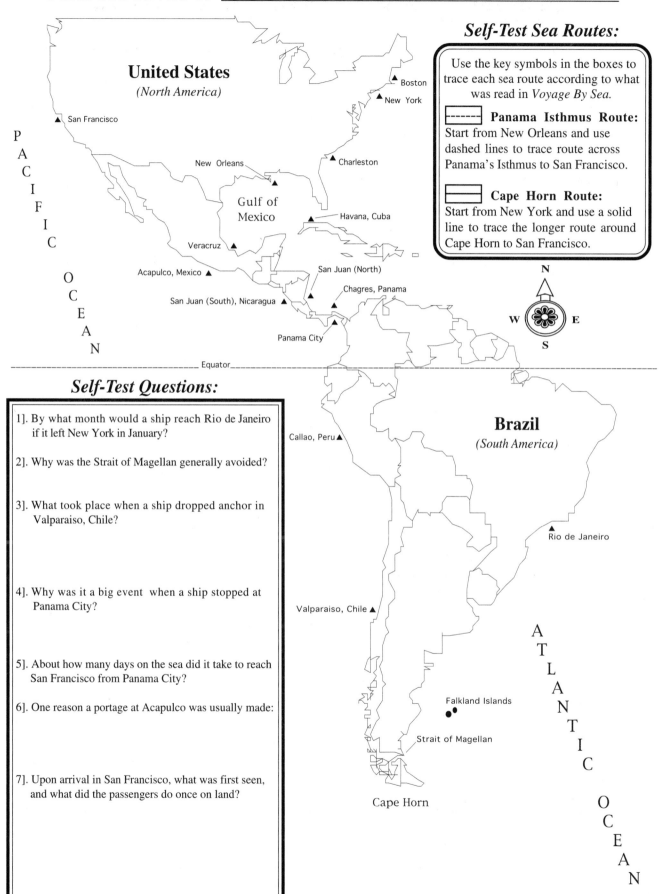

United States
(North America)

▲ Boston
▲ New York

▲ San Francisco

P
A
C
I
F
I
C

O
C
E
A
N

New Orleans

Gulf of
Mexico

▲ Charleston

▲ Havana, Cuba

Veracruz ▲

Acapulco, Mexico ▲

San Juan (North)

San Juan (South), Nicaragua ▲

Chagres, Panama

Panama City

Equator

Self-Test Sea Routes:

Use the key symbols in the boxes to trace each sea route according to what was read in *Voyage By Sea*.

Panama Isthmus Route:
Start from New Orleans and use dashed lines to trace route across Panama's Isthmus to San Francisco.

Cape Horn Route:
Start from New York and use a solid line to trace the longer route around Cape Horn to San Francisco.

N
W E
S

Self-Test Questions:

1]. By what month would a ship reach Rio de Janeiro if it left New York in January?

2]. Why was the Strait of Magellan generally avoided?

3]. What took place when a ship dropped anchor in Valparaiso, Chile?

4]. Why was it a big event when a ship stopped at Panama City?

5]. About how many days on the sea did it take to reach San Francisco from Panama City?

6]. One reason a portage at Acapulco was usually made:

7]. Upon arrival in San Francisco, what was first seen, and what did the passengers do once on land?

Callao, Peru ▲

Brazil
(South America)

▲ Rio de Janeiro

Valparaiso, Chile ▲

A
T
L
A
N
T
I
C

O
C
E
A
N

Falkland Islands

Strait of Magellan

Cape Horn

✷ JOURNEY BY LAND ✷

The promise of gold was certainly strong to lure men into crossing the expanse of varied geography that separated them from the fortunes of their dreams. Yet for thousands of argonauts who chose the land route to California in 1849, thoughts of sudden wealth would cloud over the reality of a long, difficult and sometimes deadly journey. Every type of landscape from boundless green prairie, swollen rivers, endless stretches of sage covered plains, hot sandy deserts, to steep rugged mountains would first have to be crossed in order to reach the gold fields. Nevertheless, with gold beckoning on the western horizon, these adventurers were not clearly focused on just how demanding their trip would be. Rather, their thoughts were concentrated on what supplies and mining tools could be loaded onto the wagons in anticipation of the earliest possible departure for a trip that would last four to six months.

The 2000 mile journey across half the continent usually began in May when spring grasses were tall enough for livestock to graze. Goldseekers mainly set out from one of two Missouri cities: Independence or St. Joseph, which at the time were considered the frontier of civilization that marked the boundary to the open west. These towns were full of activity with hundreds of anxious fortune-hunters arriving daily by foot, wagons or steamboats. Businesses were selling every imaginable kind of need or want, and to be sure, the streets were filled with many people from far away places. With the exception of occasional accidents and deaths, especially from disease, that would shadow the men, women and children all the way to California, a scene of excitement and talk of hoped-for riches was everywhere.

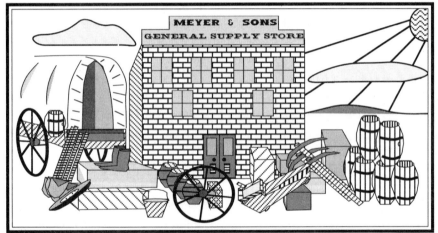

Before venturing out, almost all of the goldseekers organized themselves into the safety of a group known as a **company**. These partnerships consisted of small parties to upwards of more than 60 members. Collectively they pooled their funds to buy supplies and outfit the assembly of wagons and animals needed to haul their belongings. Wagons were generally pulled by mules or oxen which were more durable than horses under stressful conditions. Horses were also used but mainly by riders scouting paths or campsites ahead of the wagon train. Foods such as dried beef and fruit, bacon, beans, rice, flour, sugar and coffee were also purchased. These basic provisions, in addition to some hunting, would sustain them for the duration of their long journey. They agreed as well to share necessary responsibilities of labor such as guard duty and the management of animals this challenging trip demanded.

Once a company was ready to roll there was a choice of trails the '49ers could take west. But it was the Emigrants' Trail (also called the Oregon-California Trail) and its many cutoffs that was most traveled because it was the fastest, most direct land route to the gold fields for the majority of argonauts who headed west in 1849.*

*Modern states will be used throughout this segment for clarity. Only unorganized territories existed west of Missouri at this time with the exception of Texas which became a state in 1845. Paths had been opened to Oregon and California by the late 1830s, and news of available farmland encouraged others to follow. In 1844 the first successful wagon train entered California, and many new cutoffs were being explored as well. There were also several southern roads via Mexico to California, but this book focuses on only one popular trail taken in 1849. See map on page 36 to preview the general land route before continuing.

*From St. Joseph, the heavily loaded wagons first had to traverse the Missouri River which would be one of many such crossings. There were no bridges built this far west at the time, so wagons were carried over for a fee on flat wooden boats called ferries. Most of the animals were simply tethered to the craft and swam across. Drownings of both men and animals were not uncommon, but once regrouped on the other side, the companies rolled northwest until they reached the Big Blue River which they followed through Kansas to Nebraska on a trail where few trees grew, and the wide continuous grasslands of the open prairie spread out. Since trees were scarce, the travelers used "**buffalo chips**" for fuel to cook their meals. Without natural cover, they were exposed to the violent lightning and thunderstorms that prevailed in the May and June skies of late spring; their only protection from the elements was limited to the singular enclosures of wagons and leaky tents. The animals fared much worse: being completely in the open, they were often mercilessly pelted and injured by large hailstones.

As the long broken lines of wagons passed each other across the Nebraska prairie, deep scars were made in a confusion of trails. The companies were now traveling through Indian territory and from time to time watched with shock and wonder by Native Americans who survived off this land. Most Indians simply wanted to trade with the

Prairie grass in Nebraska. F. P. A. Photo

emigrants for items they deemed useful such as gunpowder, clothing or food. Some desired to barter for trinkets that suited their fancy. Still, many of the goldseekers looking on saw only a threat and prepared for the worst.

An Indian assault was unusual and generally only occurred if a small group was isolated, but the passing emigrants were still fearful and most everyone carried a gun. Ironically this led to a majority of injuries and deaths being inflicted on themselves by mishandling weapons. In the evening, wagon trains were often formed in a circle, but not because they were waiting for an attack as many commonly believe today. It was made to create a temporary corral in order to keep their animals from wandering off in the night or being stolen. As the journey progressed, Indian fears would be the least of their worries.

Many companies used a guidebook written by Joseph E. Ware who had never made the actual trip west. Full of inaccuracies, he compiled known information about the trail, and made up other parts on hearsay. Attempting the journey himself in 1849, he became ill and was deserted by his company where he died by the wayside several days later.

Eventually the prairie connected with the Platte River: a meandering length of muddy water and constant companion for hundreds of miles through Nebraska and Wyoming. It led to the gradually rising sage-covered plains that would guide them toward the entrance of the Rockies. At this point the appearance of backtrackers who had given up the journey were observed less frequently. It was also a time for raised spirits when natural landmarks were seen. The first was Courthouse Rock, quickly followed by the weathered spire of Chimney Rock—next was Scotts Bluff. All slowly emerged in the distance as the emigrants monitored their progression west.

Emigrants' Trail landmark Chimney Rock, Nebraska.

Spectacular stretches of scenery filled their eyes as companies ventured far beyond familiar civilization until they reached United States military outposts. Fort Laramie in eastern Wyoming was one such welcomed encounter and provided the emigrants with an opportunity to buy supplies, send letters home, make repairs and rest under the security of the calvary.

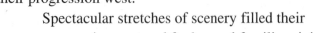

'49er names etched on Independence Rock, Wyoming.

Beyond the fort, companies continued to follow the Platte's westward lead. But after weeks of travel on this dependable watercourse it too was left behind. From here they set out across an arid basin where they soon joined with their next major water source—the Sweetwater River. It was along this stream that the lone recognizable shape of Independence Rock came into view. The widely praised whale-shaped feature was named so because many wagon trains made it to this juncture around the 4th of July. Thousands of '49ers camped here and recorded their presence by prominently etching their names into the large stone monument.

*The long drive was generally routine other than crossing a deep gully or passing the isolated graves of unfortunates who died in accidental shootings, wagon mishaps, or even murders. But more commonly, disease such as **cholera** took the heaviest toll on the emigrants' lives. Water was plentiful, and fresh meat such as buffalo and antelope could be shot on the hoof. Travel across the gentle sandy plain of this vast land was almost misleadingly easy thus far, but that would rapidly begin to change.

This song summed up the feelings of many '49ers crossing the plains:

You calculate on sixty days to take you over the plains.
For there you'll lack for bread and meat for coffee and for brains.
Your sixty days are a hundred or more, your grub you've gotta divide.
*Your steers and mules are **alkalized**, so foot it you cannot ride.*
There's not a log to make a seat along the river Platte,
So when you eat you've gotta stand or sit down square and flat.
Its fun to cook with buffalo chips, take one that's newly born,
If I knew once what I know now, I'd have gone around the Horn!

Even today wheel ruts in the original trail remnants can be seen. Additionally, multitudes of animals dropped manure in front of the wagons they pulled which makes their path especially noticeable in grassland areas since it grows taller than the surrounding vegetation.

The companies continued on the Sweetwater throughout central Wyoming for much of July. Having had many days of good water and grass for the animals, the river was about to give way to the rise of the Rocky Mountains. South Pass was the natural access over the gradual hump of this towering barrier that separated the sources of east and west flowing rivers. It was not especially steep where they crossed, but the coarse rugged trail, freezing nights, and patches of snow that crowned the distant alpine summits of this pine-treed highland made their gain in elevation clear. They paid for this easy passage over the **continental divide** by exposing themselves to a quickly shifting climate where billowing, anvil-sculpted storm clouds gathered on the surrounding heights between crystal blue skies.

Changeable as the weather conditions could be, the companies would be changing too as they rattled across the landscape. Many companies who had once massed together now began to separate from each other as they gained altitude. Groups that had lightened their overloaded wagons earlier left behind companies who stubbornly held on to all of their possessions. But as team animals strained under the excessive weight, the decision to eliminate property became a necessity. The trail side was literally an open store with items such as storage trunks, clothing, tools, books, iron-cast pots, and multitude of discarded personal belongings that were no longer considered important.

It was in the mountains that cholera mysteriously disappeared, probably because of cooler temperatures, but death for other various reasons was still commonplace. Grave markers were daily reminders of the danger along the trampled sage of the dusty road. But more immediate concerns demanded attention throughout this broad, expansive plain that was filled with bumpy ups and downs of ridges and canyons, harmful alkalized springs, and perilous river crossings. The difficulties of travel continued to increase over the next variety of miles as wagons pushed deeper into this unfamiliar continent.

The emigrants were still on the regular, well-traveled road up to this point. But not far from South Pass, the first of several mile-reducing cutoffs was encountered by the '49ers. Most companies chose to leave the main trail, and took the northwesterly path named Sublette's Cutoff; their success with this timesaving branch led emigrants to attempt a second major cutoff—Hudspeth's: this fork guided the wagons to southern Idaho's Steeple Rocks where they dipped southwest into Nevada.* By leaving the main route, they bypassed the frontier trading post of Fort Bridger, and a trail option that led to the Mormon stronghold of Salt Lake City, Utah. But west of that city, the nearly waterless desert salt flat of Hasting's Cutoff would have to be crossed, and few considered this loop to be the best path to California in 1849.**

Rough terrain and little-known cutoffs challenged the resolution of the emigrants as they climbed and descended the mountain passes of the Rockies. Mules, oxen, and horses of the wagon trains still had to be fed and watered, and this became increasingly troublesome. The most popular campsites were often overused by previous companies: grasses were all but gone, and watering places surrounded with an assortment of broken wagon parts, casks of spoiled meat, chains, pieces of harnesses, broken glass and a variety of other debris. Many times it would be necessary for a company to travel out of their way to find suitable feed for their animals who were slowly becoming malnourished and overworked.

*Steeple Rocks was named so because of the steeple-like formations that reminded some of churches. The area is known today as the City of Rocks.
**California travelers in 1849 were still reeling from the Donner Party tragedy of 1846-47 who chose Hasting's Cutoff via the desert route south of Great Salt Lake. Due to lost time, a variety of complicating circumstances and plain bad luck they became snowbound in the Sierra just north of Lake Tahoe where some resorted to cannibalism in order to survive.

*By mid August the '49ers reached a pivotal lifeline on their journey—the Humboldt River in Nevada. Temperatures easily passed the century mark in this wide, elevated, sage-speckled desert basin that was appealingly contrasted in the far distance by mountainous snowbound pinnacles. Emigrants frequently complained about the poor quality of water, and the thin, flimsy firewood provided by the dense groves of willows along the Humboldt, but they also must have recognized how dependent they were on its gifts; passage would have been nearly impossible without it.

As the companies advanced along the river's sandy trail, its powdery mixture of small, jagged pieces of abrasive rock methodically cut and split the hooves of animals causing them much discomfort. Adding to the misery of scorching heat, loose sand, and thick blinding dust, the Humboldt's many twists and turns forced tiresome detours away from the river which made travel extremely frustrating. These conditions quickly took their toll on the goldseekers. At this stage tempers often flared, but the argonauts dealt with their situation as best they could. All were inescapably bound to the Humboldt's meandering thread of life-giving water, and they would be for many days to come.

The emigrants traveled nearly 300 miles of this oasis-like waterway watching it gradually become more sluggish and shallower with each passing day. The river also became increasingly impregnated with concentrations of alkali which gave it a milky-green color and made it almost undrinkable. No one had ever thought a river could just disappear in the sand, but like a cruel joke the Humboldt was, in fact, slowly draining into a sink where it evaporated into scum beneath a blazing desert sun farther west. But 100 miles before the Humboldt terminated, a large area of patchy grasslands known as Lassen Meadow fanned out along its banks. This last welcomed repose came at a time when both men and animals alike were in sensible need of a few days rest. And it was here a major decision about which trail to take into California had to be made before pushing on.

**An increasingly harsh geography discouraged many companies from going directly across Nevada to the end of the Humboldt. For there it was certain a 40 mile sunburnt desert would have to be crossed before inching across the Sierra near Lake Tahoe. Because of this, many companies in 1849 decided to leave the river in favor of what they were mistakenly led to believe was a shortcut to the northern California gold diggings. By making the choice to take a path named Lassen's Cutoff, they hoped to make their journey quicker and less hazardous. Unknown to the emigrants, however, this northwesterly heading would take them toward obstacles that would make their course even more demanding, and

Thistle on bank of Humboldt River, Nevada.

worse, longer. In the coming years this dangerous and lethal section would treacherously become known as the "Greenhorn" or "Death Trail."

Having covered some 1700 miles at an average of 15 a day, the elusive gold fields were still several hundred unyielding miles away. It was now early September, and a blistering hot, nearly waterless region northwest of the Humboldt awaited the emigrants. The next 33 miles harbored only two small brackish springs that were not much more than trickles; they did, however, provide a means to survive as the wagons approached Nevada's Black Rock Desert.

*This river had other names in its past, but it was renamed by explorer John C. Frémont in honor of Alexander von Humboldt who made some of the first accurate and extensive maps in the Pacific region.
**The best trail turned out to be a continuation west beyond the end of the Humboldt. From there, emigrants crossed what became known as Forty Mile Desert. This led to the Carson and Truckee Rivers where the Sierra could be traversed to the gold fields.

The treeless, sun-drenched plain leading up and away from the river was a torturous stretch. Many dead and dying beasts traced miles of this rock-ribbed mountainous pass by the time more fortunate companies had reached the second watering area named Rabbit Hole Springs. Argonauts dug a number of cavities on this spot to pool water that seeped to the surface, yet the muddied liquid held in those pits could not meet the needs of all hungry, overworked, thirst-crazed animals; the most agonized slumped to their knees, breathing heavily, eyes open wide with confusion, near death. Some companies were forced to reduce their loads once again, or had to combine their teams and supplies to one less wagon because of their loss.

Abandoned wagons and valuable articles were everywhere—much of it burned or destroyed by its owners who were frustrated with their situation. They displayed their anger by insuring that no one else would be able to use their property. After making camp around the stench of animal carcasses seething with buzzing flies and maggots, they filled their wooden casks with a scant supply of silty water and left this horrific scene with the morning light.

Bleached animal bones and rusty artifacts can still be found along the powdery desert trail of Lassen's Cutoff.

Around noon the companies descended a rough, mountainous path where they could look upon the level, white-hot sink of Black Rock Desert spanning nearly fifty miles broad. They now realized that giving in to their wrongly perceived temptation to shave off miles by taking this uncertain road, they had cast themselves into the extremity of miscalculated turmoil—practicable judgement now became the essence of their error. Into the cauldron, wagons crunched through a sagebrush plain to a barren reach of frost-colored alkali. Here, countless wheels spun storm-like plumes of dust that choked the intensely hot and distorted air above the dry-baked crust of the desert trail. Everything was submerged in suffocating ashy clouds of bitter tasting grit that even made breathing an effort. The emigrants hurried across this indifferent landscape which took its toll on the hard-worn animals who were allowed little rest.

Travel during the night was often preferred to escape the searing heat, and everyone able to walk did so to help ease the burden pulled by their thirsty, footsore animals whose mouths foamed under the stressful conditions. Exhausted mules or oxen that collapsed in their harnesses were prompted to stand and continue with calls and tugs by their drivers. When all seemed lost, drivers twisted the tails of failing animals, or used their whips in order to shock them into carrying on. If these blatantly cruel means did not encourage an animal to move, the fading creature was unhitched from the wagon with the certainty that it would die. Their ruined bodies lay strewn all across this seemingly endless desert highway where the next available water was 27 miles away. Grimly, their bloated, odorous corpses acted as quiet guideposts that kept wagons on course during night travel. But it wasn't always dead animals or discarded property that marked the way. Occasionally the emigrants were reminded of their own mortality when, in the darkness, their lanterns illuminated human remains left by those without the energy nor desire to bury their companions.

Black Rock Desert in northwestern Nevada. The trail went to the dark peak in the foreground left of center where a hot boiling spring of bad tasting sulphur smelling water was available.

Unforgiving as travel may have been since leaving the Humboldt, the companies finally made it to the next crucial water camp within this desert basin. There they saw the usual array of fallen beasts and wreckage left behind surviving animals had courageously pulled so far. Encircled by such visions, it must have been a strain to shut out this backdrop of scenery as these pioneers drank water, tea or coffee, ate a meal of hard bread, beans, rice, or maybe a rarer treat of sugar-sweetened dried apples or prunes.

The last of the deserts had been crossed by mid September, and the bulk of the emigrants' journey was behind them. Their suffering was possibly consoled by thoughts of gold and ever present conversations of home. But in the distance beyond the miles of sagebrush, the hazy blue-grey indentation of the Sierra Nevada's towering granite skyline, bearing snow-crested peaks in the highest elevations, loomed clearer and more imposing with every sunrise.

Abandoned wagons on desert. F.P.A. Photo.

By now the emigrants had reached the eastern side of California, but imagine how weary these adventurers must have been. Many never got enough to eat; their clothes were threadbare; animals were haggard, and battered wagons needed repairs. To make things even more grievous after months of travel, a new disease called **scurvy** had become visible. Some no doubt questioned if the trip was indeed worth it at this point, even though they were now very close to the fields of gold that had called them.

Continuing on Lassen's Cutoff, the companies entered a pass near the Oregon border that led to Goose Lake where they stopped to recover for a few days. When they proceeded, the trail at last headed south into the heart of California. Travel through this uplifted plain was exceptionally pleasant at first as there was abundant grass for the animals, good water, and plenty of wild game supplying

Lassen Peak in northern California. F.P.A. Photo

fresh meat. But as the '49ers made their way toward the Mother Lode, the road again became progressively difficult with each passing day as they approached the high country of the Sierra Nevada.

As they entered the final mountainous spine that blocked their goal, the route became threateningly steep, rocky, and narrow as they gained altitude. Wagons could not even pass each other through most of this pine forested course, and once again the emigrants' meager resources were severely taxed. The sides of the path were littered with the familiar sights of lifeless animals, smashed wheels, belongings and graves: these were the distressful surroundings that tested their will; simply surviving was a real concern, and many companies fragmented or broke up completely if they had not already. It was now late October and the fast changing conditions at this higher elevation might easily shift from a soaking rain to icy blasts of freezing sleet or snow. Faced with the consequences of unstable weather, argonauts moved with guarded purpose as they could be trapped or lucky to escape the granite barrier of the Sierra with nothing more than what could be carried on their backs.

The descending slope of the cutoff remained trying, but rejoicingly ended at the settlement on the eastern side of the Great Central Valley for which it had been named—Peter Lassen's Ranch. Here the exhausted goldseekers recovered from their ordeal and made future plans. After partaking in a well-deserved recuperation, necessary supplies were purchased at Lassen's, or if more convenient farther south at Sutter's Fort in Sacramento, the traditional starting point for the gold fields. Toughened by rigorous months of travel, the seasoned emigrants prepared for the reason they had come west. Rested and resupplied, the real search for gold began.

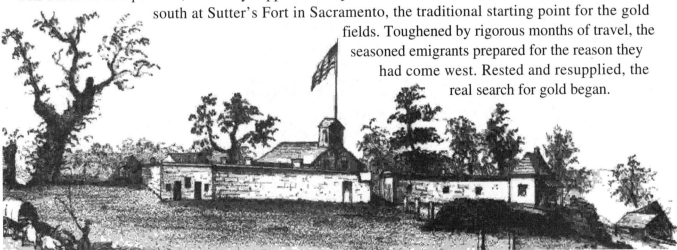

Sutter's Fort, California 1849. California State Library Archive

Self-Test: JOURNEY BY LAND

A.   An adventurer who traveled to California: A __ __ __ __ __ __ T

B.   Groups of organized wagon train members called themselves a: _____

C.   Month the journey usually began because grasses were tall enough for animals to graze: _____

D.   Two major cities where the trail west departed: _____ and _____

E.   Name the first river crossed at the start of the route: _____

F.   Reason why the Oregon-California or Emigrants' Trail was popularly used: _____

_____

G.   Animals generally chosen to pull wagons: _____

H.   Name for continuous grasslands on first leg of trip: _____

I.   Used for cooking fuel when there was no wood: _____

J.   Feared by the emigrants even though they caused little trouble: _____

K.   Major river flowing through Nebraska and Wyoming territories: _____

L.   Name any two natural landmarks that were passed: _____

M.   One reason military outposts were welcomed sights: _____

N.   Two diseases that killed or weakened many travelers: _____

O.   Mountains entered through South Pass during the month of July: _____

P.   Three reasons wagon animals died: _____

Q.   Why some emigrants went to Salt Lake City, Utah: _____

R.   Purpose wagons made a circle at night: _____

S.   Caused Humboldt River water to become nearly undrinkable: _____

T.   Average number of miles traveled each day by most goldseekers: _____

U.   Name of largest desert crossed in northwestern Nevada: _____

V.   Name six foods eaten by pioneers: _____

W.   Other names given to the dangerous Lassen Cutoff: _____

X.   Last mountains crossed to reach the California gold fields: _____

Y.   Three reasons the final mountainous stretch was difficult: _____

_____

Z.   Fort in modern day Sacramento where supplies could be purchased: _____

ACTIVITY: Write a personal diary for any three days of the six month adventure as if you were there in 1849 after rereading *Journey By Land*. Use your own paper and you can make it look "aged" by following the additional instructions below.

MAKE YOUR DIARY LOOKED AGED

A. Before you write, sponge very strong coffee or tea on your "diary pages."

B. While damp, tear off the outside page edges creating a "ragged" look, then using a candle in a safe place, singe the edges BEFORE the paper dries.

C. When dry, complete your diary using black or brown ink to add realism.

MAP ACTIVITY: *JOURNEY BY LAND TO CALIFORNIA*

The map below shows the 2000 mile **Emigrants' Trail via Lassen's Cutoff** from Missouri to Sutter's Fort, California. Do the following: **1)**. Starting from St. Joseph or Independence, use a highlighter to *trace the route marked with numbers and letters* as described in *Journey By Land*. **2)**. *Label Famous Landmarks "A through E"* in the box on the lines provided. Use the drawings below to match each landmark on the trail. **3)**. **Complete the "Diary Box."** Imagine you are traveling to California in 1849. Start by choosing any one of the seven *region numbers*: they indicate various geographical locations along the trail such as prairie, mountains, deserts or plains. Also be sure to *record the approximate month* you would have been at your location. Then, *briefly describe one observation* such as your health, a campsite, weather or landmark referred to in *Journey By Land*. **4)**. Finally, *label each outlined state*; use an atlas if needed.

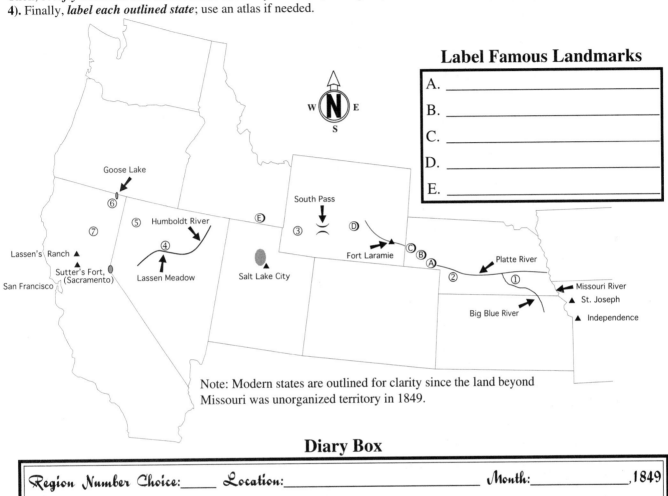

Label Famous Landmarks

A. _____

B. _____

C. _____

D. _____

E. _____

Note: Modern states are outlined for clarity since the land beyond Missouri was unorganized territory in 1849.

Diary Box

Region Number Choice:_____ Location:_____ Month:_____,1849

Dear Diary, _____

_____

_____

_____

_____

_____

_____

FAMOUS LANDMARK DRAWINGS

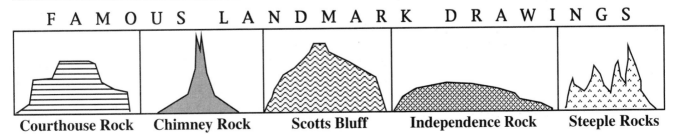

Courthouse Rock   **Chimney Rock**   **Scotts Bluff**   **Independence Rock**   **Steeple Rocks**

WHERE GOLD IS FOUND ✦

Gold is a very dense mineral that weighs about 19 times more than the weight of water. Since gold is heavy, it will rarely be found on top of lighter materials such as sand or gravel and is often hidden beneath the surface just out of sight.

Bits and pieces of loose gold can be located in an assortment of places where water and gravity have deposited them, but the source of the element can most often be traced to a type of rock called **quartz**. This is where gold forms when chemical and volcanic conditions are just right.

Over the years the easiest gold, no doubt, has been discovered but that doesn't mean an occasional lucky strike can't be made today; it's out there if one knows where to look.

For instance, a man who lived in a Mother Lode town along Highway 49 was simply walking with his dog by the edge of a stream when he noticed by chance a nugget lodged between a split rock as he ambled along its bank.

Heavy rainfall likely exposed his find from its ancient hiding place within the hillside. Gravity then forced it to a low point within reach of high water. From there it was swept along before becoming trapped in streambed rocks. As the water level receded, the treasure laid within eyeshot of the unwitting, not to mention fortunate, **prospector**.

The price of gold at the time was $350 an ounce (his weighed 2). Needless to say it was a great day for walking the dog!

Carefully examine the drawing "*Where Gold is Found*," and who knows, maybe you may have a bit of "Forty-Niner" luck one day.

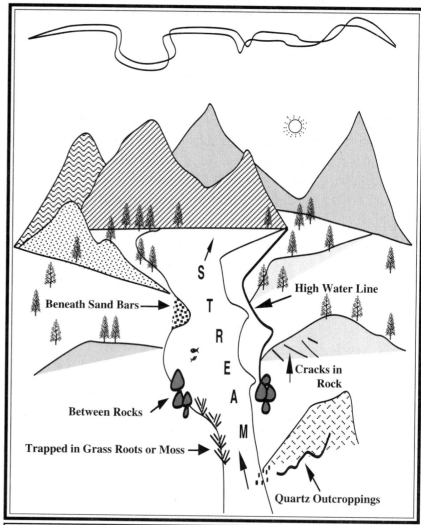

Beneath Sand Bars
High Water Line
Cracks in Rock
Between Rocks
Trapped in Grass Roots or Moss
Quartz Outcroppings

♣ ——— Self-Test ——— ♠

After reading *Where Gold Is Found* and examining the drawing, list the six places it can be located then answer questions A and B.

1. _____   2. _____
3. _____   4. _____
5. _____   6. _____

A. Why won't gold nuggets ever be found on top of sand? _____

B. A gallon container of water weighs 8 pounds, how much would the same container of gold weigh?
    (Hint multiply) _____

37

Separating loose gold from sand and gravel was a ever-present challenge that led to a variety of mining methods during the California Gold Rush and beyond. The earliest tools used by fortune-seekers were simple yet practical instruments designed to screen the abundant **placer gold** from the material it was mixed within. Each device attempted to make gold removal faster, but more effective equipment was always being tested and developed. Over time, after the easiest gold had been taken, inventive miners created the most powerful and sophisticated breakthroughs, namely, hydraulic cannons and mechanical dredgers. Those two methods made it possible to efficiently extract even the tiniest bits of yellow metal embedded in gravel that was all but impossible to remove by physical labor alone.

Gold fused inside solid rock posed another set of problems for miners. But just like placer mining, it was resourcefulness and technology that progressively led to more efficient gold removal techniques in this arena as well. Known as **hardrock mining**, it too went through a series of transitions before more complex machinery made it possible to effectively crush the huge quantities of **ore** needed to make it profitable. But like all large-scale mining operations of the past, there was an environmental cost.

Although the prospectors of old were the first to sift through the untouched gold deposits of the Mother Lode, they never found it all. Modern goldseekers using the same fundamental methods of bygone days regularly wash out "color" trapped in their pans or riffle bars. And as in the past, anyone who has ever uncovered a sparkling flake of gold shares the timeless thrill and common experience that has fueled countless dreams of hoped-for wealth hidden just beneath the surface.

Can you name the four mining methods shown below in this drawing and explain how each one works?
If not, read the following section describing the various tools used to extract gold during the Gold Rush and beyond.

California State Library Archive

Placer Mining

Gold that has weathered away and broken free from the rock that once held it is the easiest kind of gold to find. During the rush and to this day placer gold can be discovered and retrieved from just about any "place" gravity carries it to rest, thus the name. Miners knew that placer gold was once naturally bonded within a type of rock called quartz which had been loosened from its original source over time by the forces of nature. Being heavy, the gold gathered under lighter gravels and cracks in bedrock when the force of gravity and water could no longer carry it. Getting it was still backbreaking work, but almost every goldseeker was assured enough flakes and nuggets to subsist in the earliest days of the Gold Rush using the right tools.

Each placer mining technique served to make the removal of gold mixed in sand and gravel easier and less labor intensive. And on the following pages it will become clear that with American ingenuity, the simplest method of recovering placer gold soon developed into more efficient and sophisticated devices over a relatively short period time.

PANNING

Many methods were employed to expose free gold, but panning is the most basic. All a prospector required was a pan, shovel, pick and knife to scour out the places where gravity caused the precious metal to collect. To begin, a miner had to shovel deep into the bottom of a likely pocket of sandy gravel or scrape the contents of mud and roots from between rocks he picked apart. Adding water to the mixture in his rusted pan made it possible to swirl the contents around and around allowing the lighter materials to slosh out while the heavier gold remained at the bottom. As the assortment of sediments disappeared, a final delicate tilt of the pan's lip allowed the last bits of fine silt to spill over the edge leaving behind only black sand, gleaming flakes of yellow or maybe a nugget.

The process of panning was tedious, strenuous and time consuming. Experienced prospectors chiefly used this method in order to quickly survey an area before they staked a claim and set up more efficient equipment. Skill and patience would usually yield him at least four to $20 a day from the icy water during the prime of the Gold Rush; but it was still laborious work, and few ever hit it rich with a pan. Nonetheless, miners who exhaustively panned their hard-won profits reaped a measure of California's wealth. Their earnings eventually ending up with an **assayer** who determined the gold's value and melted it down into bars for easy shipment to west and east coast banks.

California State Library Archive

39

ROCKER

A faster technique of sifting through gold-bearing gravels quickly caught on during the rush and could be seen along every stream in the Mother Lode. Known as the rocker or "cradle" since it resembled a baby's bed, it operated on the same principle as panning but provided miners with the advantage of being able to wash out more material in a day.

This process worked particularly well if two men cooperated. One would gather buckets of gravel where gold was likely to hide while the other dumped the contents into the hopper that had holes punched in a thin sheet of metal on the bottom. Water was then poured on the muddy contents with a dipper while the handle on the hopper was rapidly shaken back and forth causing all but the largest pieces of the mix to drop on an angled frame stretched over with canvas. Called an "apron," fine bits of gold would be trapped on the canvas while larger pieces of gold and debris slipped to the bottom of the rocker through a gap at the end of it.

As the rocking continued, water would flush the remaining material over a series of evenly spaced wooden barriers known as riffle bars. Their purpose was to allow lighter sands and gravels to spill over the tops of the riffles and out the end while the heavier gold was trapped behind the bars where it would be collected several times a day.

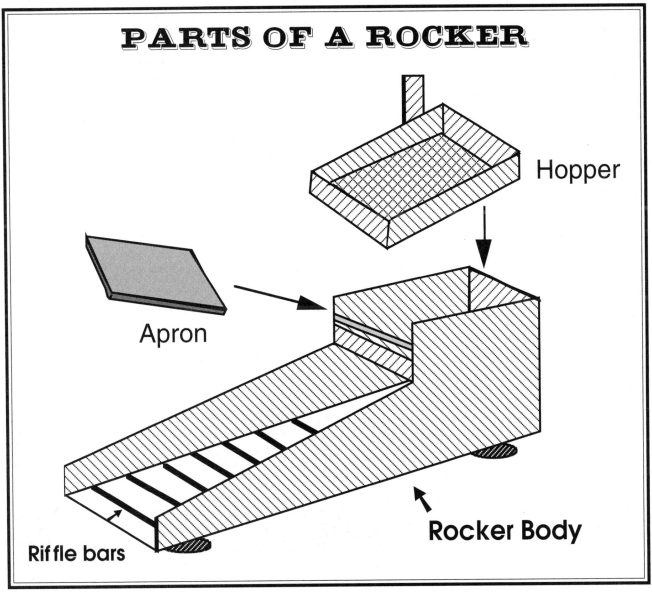

PARTS OF A ROCKER

Hopper

Apron

Rocker Body

Riffle bars

40

LONG TOM

There were other gold strikes in the United States before 1848 and one of the largest was in Georgia. When the rush began in California, experienced miners from that state brought knowledge that made the task of washing gold from ever larger quantities of gravels even more effective.

The "long tom" as it was known, worked like a rocker except a constant flow of water diverted from a stream was channeled through a canvas hose into a trough called the "tom." Muddy sands and gravels dug up were poured in the trough and then agitated with a

Notice canvas hose that directed a constant flow of water into the long tom.

California State Library Archive

shovel. This caused the smaller bits of gold and other material to fall with water through half-inch holes drilled in a metal plate at the bottom of the widening end of the tom. Known as a "riddle," it separated the larger, coarser waste rock making it easy to remove. The filtered sediments that spilled below the riddle flowed over another trough with riffle bars. Here the brass-colored metal was trapped while the quickly moving water washed away most other fragments of rock, sand and mud.

SLUICE BOX

Another mining improvement was the sluice box. Brought to the foothills of the Sierra by the Brazilians of South America, they had long since used this simple device. In this method, an assembly of boards were nailed together forming a trough or **flume** to which regularly spaced riffle bars were attached to the bottom. A strong, continuous rush of water was then directed over the inclined box. This helped propel the material thrown into the sluice as the force of water tumbled it over the gold-catching riffles. It was here, that the heavier gold nuggets, scales and particles would eventually be trapped behind the bars while allowing the lighter waste mud and rock to exit through the end.

Often long sections of these boxes were connected together so that a team of miners working side by side could shovel in and rake through a large quantity of gold-bearing rubble. By working in unison, miners increased their odds of making this type of placer mining very profitable by processing a greater volume of material that no one man could have done alone.

riffle bar

SECTION OF A SLUICE BOX

41

HYDRAULIC MINING

Hydraulic mining was born in California. It began in 1852 when a French-Canadian named Antoine Chabot devised a hand-sewn canvas hose to wash loose, muddy gold-bearing gravels into his sluice box. A year later an American, Edward Mattison, refined the developing method by adding a metal nozzle to the end of a similar hose. His improvement created a punch of water that was able to blast away at the much harder gold-bearing sediments of ancient riverbeds locked inside hills.

By the early 1860s crude canvas and rawhide hoses had been replaced with riveted sections of heavy iron pipes. Starting out at a diameter of thirty inches and decreasing to twelve or less over its length, this system harnessed the water's incredible power. A thick metal cannon-like end piece called a **monitor**

California State Library Archive

or "giant" with an outlet of up to eight inches was attached by way of a swivel-neck completing this relatively Spartan device. Water trapped in a reservoir at a higher elevation and the opening of a valve allowed the force of gravity to propel the available supply of liquid energy through the penstock (pipeline) that snaked down a hill. The concentration of water that violently erupted from the monitor smashed away at hidden gravel deposits creating a muddy sludge called "**slickens**" which was washed into long sluice boxes. About once a month or so millions of tiny gold particles trapped behind hundreds of riffle bars would be collected and melted into ingots (bars) that were sold at the current market price.

To aim the monitor an operator simply pulled a long wood or metal handle attached to the ball-jointed end nozzle. Since it was counterbalanced by the force of the water, pushing or pulling on the handle easily rotated the monitor in the desired direction with as little effort as it would take to close a car door. Although the monitor was easy to control, it could be very deadly if a man or animal crossed its lethal path more than two-hundred feet away! So powerful was the discharge of water that exploded from these giants, that a man striking the dynamic jet with a crowbar could not penetrate it. The force of energy was so great that boulders weighing more than 100 pounds were tossed about like enormous Ping-Pong balls. It is little wonder sediments almost as tough as concrete were efficiently splashed away with great speed by the swirling sheets of liquid that liberated the gold within.

Millions of gallons of water were needed to power the monitors. In addition to natural lakes, streams and miles of ditches, the construction of dams to make reservoirs were crucial to tap the vast quantities of liquid necessary for hydraulic mining operations. This led to the creation of dozens of water companies who controlled the reserves of potential power they sold to mines and saw mills. Eventually some of these companies extended their services to the agricultural lands of the Great Central Valley making large-scale irrigation possible. With the development of hydroelectric generators, the canals and reservoirs were quickly converted to fit the needs of a new and inexpensive source of power—electricity. This network of controlled water provided the tap for convenient, ready-made energy for the people of foothill and valley towns, even before more progressive cities like San Francisco were completely outfitted with the new technology.

Hydraulic mining was very economical. If an outfit earned only a few cents worth of gold from a piece of ground that would fill a bathtub, it was profitable. Unfortunately, this type of mining had disastrous effects on the environment. Massive areas of land were scarred into lifeless open pits and rendered useless for any other purpose. Muddy sludge that passed over the sluice boxes had to end up somewhere, and it was usually a river. Cloudy sediments replaced the once clean, free-flowing water of most major streams in the northern and southern mining districts as masses of thick, brown debris filled their channels.

The long-term consequences of hydraulic mining were unmistakable. River boat travel was impaired on notable rivers such as the Yuba and Feather; fish were suffocated and animal habitats devastated. When spring snow melt added more water to the already mud-choked riverbeds, they overflowed and destroyed choice farmlands or flooded whole communities in the lower elevations. Each year river bottoms filled ever higher with silt guaranteeing an inevitable annual flood. Catastrophe awaited valley towns situated near the paths of rivers that carried hydraulic waste. Soon the voice of public outrage slowly gathered strength putting the effects of miner's profits at odds with the livelihoods of farmers and townspeople.

A long legal battle over the issues that hydraulic mining had on the environment and communities ended in 1884 when Judge Lorenzo Sawyer ruled that the use of these powerful hoses would have to stop unless waste materials could be contained. This decision resulted in the closure of all but a handful of hydraulic operations in the coming years. Today, the many scars that these water cannons left behind remain as permanent signposts on the countryside forever marking this turbulent time.

Business end of a once active monitor used at Knickerbocker Flat near Columbia.

DREDGING

Countless tiny grains of placer gold remained deep within the hard to reach sediments of ancient Mother Lode riverbeds. The problem, however, was to develop a reliable method of scooping up or dredging huge quantities of these gravels, separate the gold and make a profit. An attempt was made as early as 1850 when a crude, steam powered dredge named the *Phoenix* was outfitted with a chain of buckets and put to use on the Yuba River near Marysville. But the endeavor failed as it suffered continuous machinery problems. Other attempts would follow with similar disappointing outcomes. High costs, low earnings, and technological complexities yet to be improved upon would hold dredging in the background for nearly half a century.

California State Library Archive

The earliest dredges that had any success were used in New Zealand in the 1860s, but it would be many years of trial and error before the Golden State would see its first profitable dredge. Eventually borrowed ideas, advancements in technology and large sums of invested money helped create California's first dependable, highly mechanized dredge in 1898. The new steam powered vessel scraped out the rich placer deposits of the Feather River near Oroville with excellent results. In the coming years, these massive, boxy processing plants became more and more common as the chains that linked a series of buckets retrieved millions of dollars in gold from river gravels throughout the state. And as technology progressed, steam was replaced by electrical power in 1901 as ever larger dredges with an impressive array of screeching metal parts evolved.

These noisy machines were by far the most complicated method of placer mining. They worked essentially like giant mechanical sluice boxes sifting through tons of hidden gravel deposits

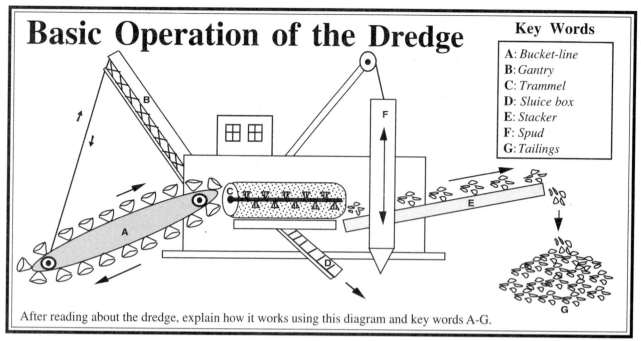

Basic Operation of the Dredge

Key Words

A: *Bucket-line*
B: *Gantry*
C: *Trammel*
D: *Sluice box*
E: *Stacker*
F: *Spud*
G: *Tailings*

After reading about the dredge, explain how it works using this diagram and key words A-G.

for the invisible bits of yellow metal that all added up to huge profits. They came in a variety of sizes and all worked basically the same, but it was the largest ones that attracted the most attention. A typical gigantic dredge was nearly 300 feet long from end to end, about 50 feet wide and stood some 75 feet above the water level at its highest point. Its internal frame was built of iron but the outside was covered with wood panels or sheet metal. Some weighed 4000 tons! These raft-like processors searched for gold by scooping up massive amounts of buried mud, sand and rocks with a revolving ladder called a *bucket-line*, some of which had 135 scoop buckets interlocked together in a rotating chain. Each thick, heavy iron bucket weighed two tons and could hold about the capacity of a regular bathtub. But most importantly, a bucket had to deliver six cents worth of gold from the watery muck to be considered profitable.

The bucket-line was supported by an iron hoist called a *gantry* which made it possible to adjust the digging angle down to a depth of up to 125 feet if needed. Amazingly these monoliths only required four men on board to operate. However, a larger support crew was also on duty ready to inspect, repair and keep the machinery in working order.

California State Library Archive

These immense floating structures had to be stabilized when in use, and it was done in simple but ingenious ways. Cables mounted to winches on the front and rear of the dredge were connected to land. They could be tightened or loosened permitting it to move sideways or forward. Additionally, a large cable-controlled spike called a *spud*, which was a hollow 60 foot iron stake located toward the back of the dredge, locked it in position while digging. With everything in place, the bucket-line rotated as the machine slowly dug from side to side sitting in its own self-made pond. New territory was accessed by loosening the cables and raising the spud which allowed the entire structure to waddle forward so another section could be excavated.

When the bucket-line delivered its muddy contents to the main body, the interior of the dredge was designed to efficiently separate gravel and gold like a huge washing machine. Scooped-up rocky sludge was first channeled into a large, oblong, open-ended barrel called a *trammel* made of heavy-duty iron pierced with thousands of quarter inch holes. Mounted horizontally at a slight angle, it constantly rotated straining smaller material past its multitude of openings. A high pressure water pipe suspended through the center of the cylinder assisted the process by blasting the disorderly mixture with powerful jets of liquid. After being rinsed, the waste rocks that tumbled to the end of the trammel were carried off on a long conveyor belt called a *stacker*. This arm extended well behind the dredge depositing great mounds of rubble known as **tailings**; the telltale signature that a dredge has worked an area.

Mud, pebbles, sand and gold that filtered through the small holes of the drum-like trammel was flushed by thousands of gallons of water while passing over an enormous maze of riffle bars and flat copper plates coated with **mercury**. This system trapped the heaviest golden flakes but also made it possible to snag even the tiniest microscopic particles known as "flour" gold. Muddy waste material that passed over the network of screens flowed out an exit in the side of the dredge returning to the watery pit where it sat. About once a week the millions of captured gold fragments would be removed and processed on the spot into 30 pound bars in preparation to be sold to the United States Mint.

Dredges were not limited to riverbeds; they could function anywhere the water table was near the surface. But after a region was exhausted of its riches, all of the topsoil was displaced and only mounds of bare rock tailings covered the landscape rendering it useless for almost any other purpose. Dredging continued throughout the 1900s reaching its peak during the 1930s. But in the following decade the government suspended all gold mining operations during World War II because they were not an essential industry to the war effort. After the war, dredging once again resumed, but the enormous operating costs and relatively low price of gold at the time were collapsing the industry.

In addition to the setback caused by the war, concerns about the environment were emerging by the 1960s. New regional laws stated that companies had to level the tailings they created and replace the topsoil of areas that were worked. This delivered a final blow for most enterprises. Today the eastern edge of the Great Central Valley is studded with the unmistakable rocky monuments left behind by the rusting hulls of these floating factories. They are still here to remind us of a specialized mining technique used to pursue mineral wealth. Dredging highlights a pinnacle of our nation's mining history that uniquely stands out from all other landscapes in our past.

Massive piles of tailings line a road near Snelling.

Hardrock Mining

When placer gold was not as easy to find, miners searched for the source of the yellow mineral that was locked inside quartz. From its earliest days, hardrock miners had to have steady nerves to bring up ore from the narrow candle lit tunnels they dug deep into the earth. The work was extremely dangerous because explosives were frequently used and the constant threat of cave-ins or fires always present. Despite the risks and expensive equipment often required for this type of mining, thousands of mine shafts were chiseled throughout the Mother Lode well beyond the prime of the Gold Rush. But after the profitable yellow-streaked rock was brought out into the light of day in wheeled carts, only half of the victory was won.

Broken chunks of ore that were carted to the surface still had to be crushed to extract the gold. Miners who could not afford costly equipment to harness water or buy steam engines to power their mills found other creative ways to grind their quartz. For example, some clever individuals simply tied a rope to the branch of a young tree that could be bent over. Then the free end of the rope was tied to a heavy, solid, iron cylinder that was positioned over pieces of ore sitting on a metal plate. By pulling hard on the rope, the iron crusher would smash the rocks as the strong, flexible tree branch made the weight easy to pull up again. The bits of crushed rock would then have to be separated by hand to get the small flakes of gold it released. Needless to say that method was not very efficient because it was time consuming, and the ore would have to be especially rich since tons would have to be crushed in order to turn a nice profit. Fortunately, there were other more practical and inexpensive techniques available to hardrock miners—knowledge brought to California by experienced goldseekers from other countries around the world.

ARRASTRA

It was the Mexicans who developed a crusher that could effectively grind a profitable quantity of ore and was available to anyone who owned a work animal. The arrastra was a simple mill that consisted of a level, circular stone floor surrounded by a low wall. A solid iron post was then mounted in the center. After a strong wooden pole was fastened horizontally to the center post like a propeller, a

heavy slice of flat rock was bolted to a chain and attached to the middle. One or two mules, hitched to the outside ends of the horizontal pole, powered the mill by walking around and around the outside wall pulling the stone slab as it crunched over finger-sized pieces of ore. Water was also added to reduce the friction of the process.

At the close of a long day for both men and animals, the grounds of pasty quartz mixed with newly released flecks of gold would be scraped up from within the basin into buckets. From here the waste was separated by washing with water or mercury, and the miner bagged his profits.

California State Library Archive

CHILEAN WHEEL

The Chileans of South America brought over their own clever idea of grinding ore too. Called the Chilean wheel, it worked exactly like the arrastra. However, instead of the animals dragging a flat slab of rock, the skilled workers from this Latin country carved a neat circular stone wheel varying from five to ten feet in diameter. The width of the wheel was about twenty-four inches, which made up the crushing surface; to this an iron ring was attached. A metal axle was then placed through a cut in the center of the heavy disk making it possible to roll. Small pieces of ore placed in front of it were then smashed as animals harnessed to wood and leather yokes pulled the wheel around and around a circular iron floor basin. The "Chile mill" was able to crush powder fine more than five tons of ore a day. And since the metal surfaces of the floor and wheel ring were very smooth, the weight of the wheel was able to efficiently release most of the prime gold held within the rock. This was a big advantage over other less precise hardrock methods.

To make the process of separating the gold from crushed rock easier, liquid mercury, also called quicksilver, was commonly utilized since it sticks to gold but not rock. As a result, it became very popular with miners who applied it to absorb the profits from their valuable grit. The combination of gold and mercury then had to be separated by boiling off the mercury. But once completed, all that was left behind was a golden reward that made it worth the effort. This process saved countless hours that would have been normally spent using only water and a sluice box to finish the same job. Although the Chilean wheel was effective, it wouldn't be too long before more advanced machines powered by steam completely dominated hardrock mining.

California State Library Archive

STAMP MILL

Although the stamp mill originated in Germany where it was put to work crushing coal, Americans during the Gold Rush improved upon the idea to extract gold from rock. This machine takes its name from the one-thousand pound metal rods or *stamp posts* with replaceable iron *shoes* that shattered ore nonstop day and night. Powered by water, California's first crude mill was operating in late 1849, but by the early 1850s, smoke from wood that fed steam boilers filled the air as hundreds of methodical stamps with noisy mechanical rattles resonated throughout the Mother Lode mashing ore. This was accomplished with a relatively simple but effective instrument.

Each machine contained a number of stamp posts known as "batteries." The smallest had only two stamps pounding away while the largest operations had 80 batteries that could crush up to 700 tons of ore in 24 hours. To power the stamps a steam engine was connected to a rubberized canvas belt that stretched around a large circular wooden disk called a *flywheel*. Attached through the center of this disk was a horizontally mounted iron drive shaft affixed to *cams*. As the flywheel revolved, cams on the drive shaft lifted and dropped the heavy stamp posts that freed rock from gold. All of this took place as operators, deafened by the orderly metallic clatter of the stamps, threw wood to the steam boiler, loaded the ore cart to fill the *hopper*, or hammered lumps of quartz held back by the *grizzly*.

These mills were furnished with baseball sized chunks of quartz from local mines which was hoisted to the top by a cable-drawn cart. When dumped, gravity and the endless medley of shaking parts led the ore down a funnel-shaped hopper where it filtered through a metal grating called a grizzly; its purpose was to stop the occasional large pieces of ore that would cause a jam in the crushing area. Ore that tumbled below the grizzly went into a water-filled trough where it was continuously pulverized by the stamps into a runny, buttermilk-colored grit called "**slurry**."

The ceaseless pounding of the stamps in the crushing area insured that the ore was thoroughly smashed releasing micro traces of gold contained in the rock. The action of the stamps splashed the

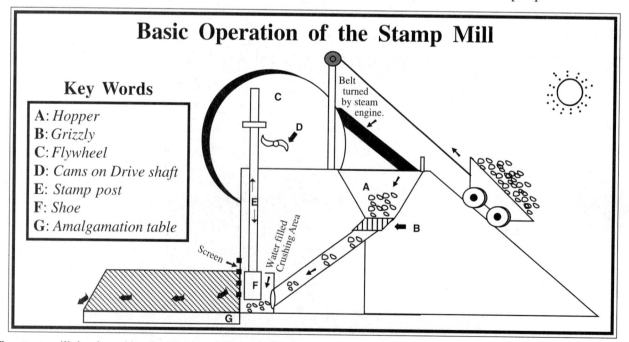

Basic Operation of the Stamp Mill

Key Words

A: *Hopper*
B: *Grizzly*
C: *Flywheel*
D: *Cams on Drive shaft*
E: *Stamp post*
F: *Shoe*
G: *Amalgamation table*

Belt turned by steam engine.

Water filled Crushing Area

Screen

The stamp mill dominated hardrock processing to modern times. It was the most efficient and cost effective way to crush ore. Modifications in design and the way they were powered changed over the years, but the basic operation principles remained.

49

water suspended particles through a fine wire screen containing 1000 holes per square inch! On the other side of the screen was a gently angled tray lined with copper. Mercury clings to gold; it also sticks to copper. So before milling began, a miner would coat a very thin film of the liquid metal onto the copper covered *amalgamation table.* This setup allowed the slurry to pass over the layer of mercury where thousands of invisible specks of once imprisoned treasure would be captured while the creamy waste material trickled off the end of the table to the tailings pile on the ground.

An experienced operator knew when to stop the mill and collect hard-won profits. For if the layer of quicksilver adhering to the copper became too loaded with gold, it would begin to break apart and slip off the table into the tailings becoming all but lost. So about once a week, as the mercury became laden with gold, the mill was shut down for a procedure known as "cleaning up." At this point the miner scraped up the heavy, clay-like, pasty mixture called **amalgam** into a ball. The dull grey silvery mass taken from the copper amalgamation table contained gold, but it still could not be seen.

After the clean up, the surface of the stamp mill's table was once again prepared with mercury, and an operator set the stamps clanking away into motion. The questionable looking glob of bonded metals that had been removed was taken away and readied to be separated with heat in a simple device known as a **retort**.

Front view of operating stamp mill located at the Mariposa History Museum.

RETORT

The final step in retrieving gold from the amalgam once it had been collected was to separate the softball-sized metallic glob by heating it in a furnace known as a retort. The process began when the amalgam was placed in a sealed chamber and heated to molten temperatures. *Since mercury vaporizes at a much lower temperature than gold, it burns off first leaving the gold behind. The evaporated quicksilver then moved through a long iron tube attached to a closed chamber cooled by water where it returned to its original form. A bucket at the end of the pipe captured the gathering droplets so it could be used again.

When the heating chamber was safe to open, an air-bubbled plug of gold resembling a sponge remained for all of the miner's time consuming work. The prize could then be refined even more by an assayer to eliminate other trace metals such as silver, copper and zinc, thus making the final bar nearly pure gold.

Retorts came in a variety of different designs, but all of them were very dangerous to use. Inhaled mercury fumes can cause numerous health problems over time ranging from liver to nerve damage among other things. Years of simply handling the substance could end in poisonous complications because it can be absorbed through the skin. Quicksilver was widely used in the early years of the Gold Rush extending into modern times as well. Its attraction to gold helped make possible the recovery of mineral wealth that otherwise would have been lost.

*Mercury vaporizes at about 700 degrees Fahrenheit and gold 3500 degrees.

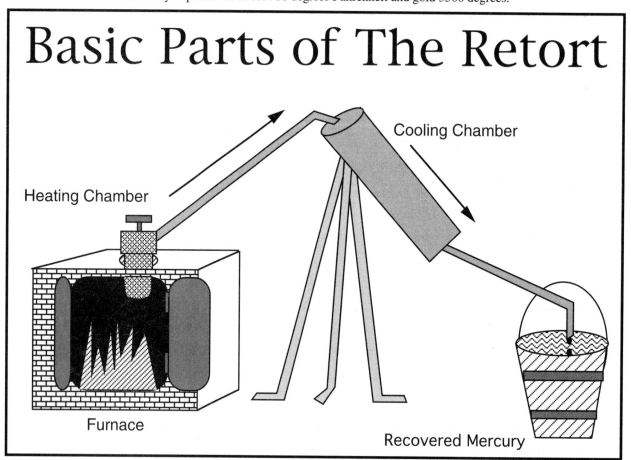

Basic Parts of The Retort

Cooling Chamber

Heating Chamber

Furnace

Recovered Mercury

A.   Name the six methods miners used to recover *placer* gold:

1.   _____   4.   _____
2.   _____   5.   _____
3.   _____   6.   _____

B.   Name three *hardrock* mining devices that crushed quartz ore:

1. _____   2. _____   3. _____

C.   Describe how a retort separates amalgam: _____

_____

_____

_____

_____

_____

D.   Write the name of the mining *instrument* that fits these words below:

1.   GANTRY: _____   5.   APRON: _____
2.   MONITOR: _____   6.   SPUD: _____
3.   FLUME: _____   7.   SLURRY: _____
4.   RIDDLE: _____   8.   SLICKENS: _____

E.   Name one of the methods you read about and explain how cooperation between miners could improve their rewards: _____

_____

_____

_____

_____

F.   Explain which mining technology was the most destructive to the environment:

_____

_____

_____

_____

_____

Mining Methods Crossword PUZZLE

ACROSS or BACKWARDS

1. Each crusher weighed 1000 pounds.

5. Another name for mercury.

6. Used a series of riffle bars to trap gold.

7. This machine left behind large piles of rock called "tailings."

8. The most basic way miners collected gold.

10. This method forced water through a "monitor."

UP or DOWN

2. A mule pulled a flat stone to crush the gold ore.

3. Gravels were channeled down a trough before they ran over the "riddle."

4. Type of rock containing gold that was crushed by a Chilean wheel.

9. Also called a cradle.

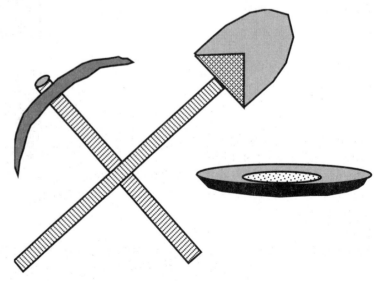

RISE & FALL of the PONY EXPRESS

"Here he comes! Away across the endless dead level of the prairie a black speck appears against the sky . . . sweeping toward us nearer and nearer . . . a whoop and a hurrah . . . a wave of the rider's hand . . . a man and a horse burst past our excited faces, and go winging away like the [last] fragment of a storm!" Thus were the words of Mark Twain upon seeing a Pony Express rider from his stagecoach heading west in 1861. It might have seemed as though this rugged type of life was glamorous, but that was rarely the case. Many of the riders were between 15 to 20 years of age and rode an average of 65 jolting miles a day changing horses about every ten miles at relay stations as they brought news to and from California.

The idea of the Pony Express began with a Missouri businessman by the name of William Russell. He knew that people in the west craved news and letters from loved ones in the east almost as much as gold. The problem was that thousands of miles separated California from the rest of the nation, and the fastest stagecoach took three weeks at best to reach the state while steamships took twice that long. Russell's solution was simple: he believed that by setting up a chain of outposts along a road nearly 2000 miles long, mail could be delivered from St. Joseph, Missouri to Sacramento, California in as little as ten days which was unheard of at the time.

To achieve his goal, Russell and his business partners hired some 80 riders and bought about 400 horses. They would be placed at 157 relay stations along a route the emigrants had been struggling through for years. In addition, stock tenders, station keepers, trail supervisors, and supply wagons were organized to support this ambitious task. The expert riders chosen for the job were young and lightweight, many under 130 pounds, and had to be willing to "risk their lives daily" for the sum of about $60 dollars a month plus bonuses. There was no shortage of riders and on April 3, 1860 the Pony Express began its first westbound run from St. Joseph with the sounds of a cheering crowd and a cannon blast.

Russell's plan was a success. The first mail reached Sacramento in just under ten days, and San Francisco letters were carried by steamboat from Sutter's Fort the following afternoon. The Express proved its worth and the faithful riders regularly dashed east and west once a week, and before long eight times a month. Californians were now all but guaranteed a closeness with the rest of the country.

This closeness did not come cheap, however. Mail was first carried at $10 an ounce. An average letter weighed about half that, but in order to compete for more business the price was later lowered to $2 an ounce. Riders carried their payload in a specially designed saddle cover called

Life-size statue of a Pony Express rider in Old Sacramento.

a "mochila" which means knapsack in Spanish. It was a rectangular shaped leather apron with pouches sewn on all four corners. The bags could be filled with a little more than twenty pounds of various letters, telegrams, and newspapers printed on tissue thin paper. Only the rider's weight held it on, so it could be whisked off in seconds for a change of horses.

As a rider traveled farther west connecting station to station, his safety became more uncertain.

This was in part because of native Paiutes living in what is now western Utah and Nevada. They were alarmed at the numbers of new people crossing over or taking their land. Relations between the natives and the settlers became hostile, and Express riders were exposed to the danger of their wrath. Equipped only with the protection of a knife and a six-shooter to keep weight at a minimum, the young riders crossed Paiute territory with nervous caution. Eventual conflicts resulted in one rider's death, several relay stations burned, and 19 other employees killed.

If Indian attack wasn't an immediate concern, the weather was another hazard that challenged the courage of the young men (and one woman). More than once, knee deep snow or swollen rivers slowed, but rarely stopped, the determination of riders crossing mountain passes and plains. In its 19 months of service, only one mochila was ever lost in over 150 demanding trips.

One of the better known riders who

Illustration of a Pony Express Mochila

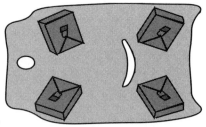

The mochila was placed on top of a feather-weight saddle.
(Actual weight of saddle and empty mochila, 13 pounds)

whisked mochilas from saddles as he rode horses across the landscape was William F. Cody. He achieved early fame during his employment with the Express by insuring the mail was relayed even though a fellow rider had been killed. Cody was quick to earn his reputation at the age of 15 and best describes his longest ride through the Rocky Mountains in his own words:

> *"One day when I galloped into Three Crossings, my home station, I found that the rider who was expected to take the trip out...had been killed; and that there was no one to take his place. I did not hesitate for a moment to undertake an extra ride of eighty-five miles [through South Pass] to Rocky Ridge, and I arrived... on time. Then, I turned back and rode to Red Buttes, my starting place...a distance of 322 miles."*

Cody later became the famous "Buffalo Bill" known for his wild west show that entertained thousands while the real west became an image of the past as towns grew and the law was enforced. But as all of the former riders aged, they surely could never forget the excitement, hardship and peril that each experienced during their brief career with the Express.

It wasn't long before the best rider and fastest horse quickly fell behind a speedier method of sending news to the west. The telegraph had been used in the eastern states and California well before 1860, but now new wires were being strung along the Express route's path. Crews working east and west were hastily connecting a transcontinental line which was to meet at Salt Lake City, Utah. By October 1861 the job was finished. Soon messages and news could be dot-dashed over geography in minutes which reduced the importance of the Express. After delivering nearly 35,000 pieces of mail, huge expenses and failure to ever make a profit ruined the diligent Pony Express.

Within a week after the completion of the Atlantic-Pacific telegraph line, the last mochila was relayed across familiar territory ending the short but famous history of the Pony Express. The San Francisco Pacific News summed up many people's feelings in a final tribute in 1861: *We have looked for you as those who wait for the morning, and how seldom did you fail us! When days were months and hours weeks, how you thrilled us out of our pain and suspense, to know the best or the worst! You have served us well!"*

SELF-TEST: PONY EXPRESS

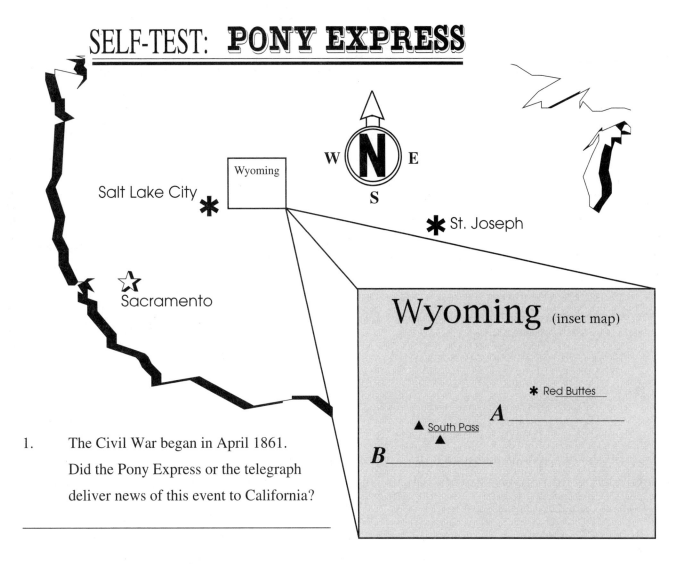

1. The Civil War began in April 1861. Did the Pony Express or the telegraph deliver news of this event to California?

_____

2. On the inset map of Wyoming, label missing relay stations on lines **A** and **B** that were part of William Cody's famous 322 mile ride.

3. Why do you think the Express chose a route through Salt Lake City? _____

_____

4. How did the many relay stations receive supplies in their far off locations? _____

_____

5. What two factors contributed to the Pony Express going out of business? _____

_____

6. The actual Pony Express route was 1,890 miles long. If each rider rode 65 miles a day, how many had to be on duty? _____(Hint: divide)   How many miles would need to be covered in 24 hours to deliver the mail in 10 days? _____(Hint: divide)

THE TRANSCONTINENTAL TELEGRAPH

In the early 1840s the telegraph began connecting states east of the Mississippi River. By the early 1850s, the growing towns of California also began sending messages with the electronic dots and dashes of a code developed mainly by Samuel B. Morse. But the large expanse of land between Fort Kearney, Nebraska all the way to Carson City, Nevada was not yet united by the technology. The services of ships, stages, and newly formed Pony Express were required to carry the bulk of all communications west. Although they filled the gap, delivery by any of those methods still could not speed information quickly enough for news hungry Californians. The only solution was to build a transcontinental telegraph that would once and for all link the vast western space separating the states.

Construction of the evenly spaced poles, wooden insulators, and bare metal wires that would span the enormous length from central Nebraska to western Nevada began in 1860. Two groups of government funded workers raced each other from opposite ends of the country setting up a single line of wires that would bring the states closer together, and finish off the bankrupt Pony Express nearly as fast. Their biggest hindrance while completing the line seemed to be replacing an occasional pole knocked over by prairie buffalo who liked pushing their one ton bodies against the lone columns to scratch themselves! In only five months, the crews made final connections on October 24, 1861 in Salt Lake City—nine months ahead of schedule.

Shortly thereafter completion, a ceremony was held in San Francisco to mark the importance of the feat. Stephen J. Field, a California judge, who took the place of the absent governor, read California's first official transcontinental message. In the midst of a crowded room a technician clicked his words on a sender that relayed them over a wire to New York in record time. Suddenly a battery powered technology made coast to coast communications a simple task that took only minutes instead of a luxury that was counted in days. Remarkably, a lone telegraph line sweeping across the countryside had swiftly changed the face of our nation.

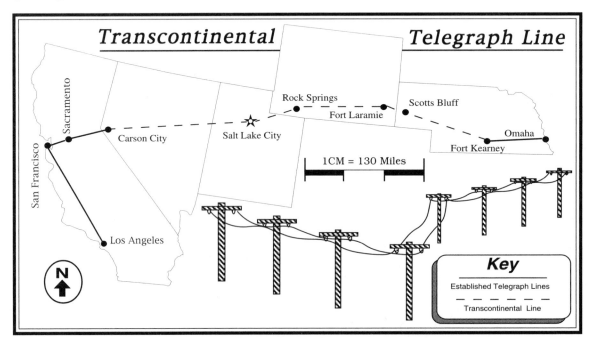

*To find out what Judge Field's first message was about, use the Morse Code Key to decipher his words on the following page:

MORSE CODE KEY

A B C D E F G H

I J K L M N O P

Q R S T U V W X

Y Z

(Decode Judge Field's Transcontinental Telegraph Message On The Lines Below)

INTRODUCTION TO TOWNS OF THE GOLD RUSH

The following pages contain a location map and brief history of over 30 representative Gold Rush towns. A majority are found along modern Highway 49 which traverses the general trail countless prospectors traveled as they wandered in search of wealth. Seemingly popping up overnight to serve the needs and entertainment desires of miners during the rush, a number of the original tent camps developed into permanent thriving communities that survive today. Yet others are decaying ghost towns, nearly forgotten place-names, or mere memories. Today, modern structures stand among remnants of slate stone walls, iron fire doors and traces of crumbling adobe foundations that have faded into ruins over tranquil decades. But these gold country settlements were also vitally linked to Central Valley and Pacific coast towns as well. They were the cornerstone supply hubs and jumping-off points; some of which became California's largest and most important cities.

The countryside between the once and still present establishments of the foothill region testifies to the heyday of the Gold Rush. Scores of abandoned mines shafts, silent remains of rusted equipment, and telltale piles of rocky debris quietly lay scattered throughout the land as they are slowly reclaimed by seasonal grasses, the sprawling branches of tall pine trees, or arching tangles of solitary oaks. There are also more mysterious reminders too.

Long stretches of mortarless stone fences painstakingly built chiefly by Chinese laborers span aimless miles of uncrowded hills over rugged territory; their nearly forgotten purpose was to mark property lines or corral livestock. Now, as in the past, a wealth of interesting sights awaits anyone with a watchful eye and desire to explore and learn. Towns within the beltway of the Mother Lode and throughout the state of California are filled with reminders of another time. Use the guide on the next page to locate each place as you read the upcoming selection, or better yet, try to visit these and other sites of interest to experience Gold Rush era history firsthand.

Guide to Towns & Locations

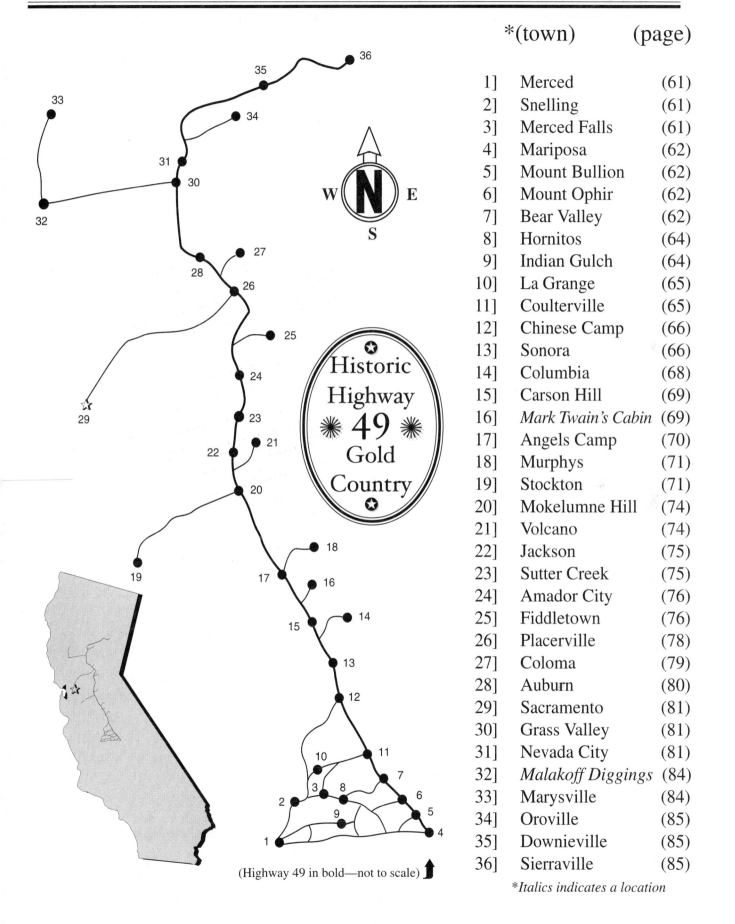

*(town)   (page)

1] Merced (61)
2] Snelling (61)
3] Merced Falls (61)
4] Mariposa (62)
5] Mount Bullion (62)
6] Mount Ophir (62)
7] Bear Valley (62)
8] Hornitos (64)
9] Indian Gulch (64)
10] La Grange (65)
11] Coulterville (65)
12] Chinese Camp (66)
13] Sonora (66)
14] Columbia (68)
15] Carson Hill (69)
16] *Mark Twain's Cabin* (69)
17] Angels Camp (70)
18] Murphys (71)
19] Stockton (71)
20] Mokelumne Hill (74)
21] Volcano (74)
22] Jackson (75)
23] Sutter Creek (75)
24] Amador City (76)
25] Fiddletown (76)
26] Placerville (78)
27] Coloma (79)
28] Auburn (80)
29] Sacramento (81)
30] Grass Valley (81)
31] Nevada City (81)
32] *Malakoff Diggings* (84)
33] Marysville (84)
34] Oroville (85)
35] Downieville (85)
36] Sierraville (85)

Italics indicates a location

Historic Highway 49 Gold Country

(Highway 49 in bold—not to scale)

MERCED

Our tour begins in the mid San Joaquin Valley which is the southern river drainage of the Great Central Valley. Shaped from a basin of natural beauty, this relatively level, semiarid plain of grasslands and wetlands was once a scene where migratory birds darkened the sky, herds of elk thousands strong roamed, immense flocks of pronghorn antelope grazed, and now extinct wolves and grizzly bears foraged. Long since altered, California's Central Valley would support farms, and its pastures nourish the domesticated animals new settlers would bring.

John Muir, the famous naturalist who helped preserve Yosemite Valley, crossed near this area in the spring of 1868 and made notes in his journal worthy of mention. He typified the region as *"One smooth, continuous bed of honeybloom, so marvelously rich that in walking from one end of it to the other... your foot would press about a hundred flowers at every step."* A bit of an exaggeration perhaps, but another who crossed this valley before Muir in its unspoiled condition also described its springtime look as *"a carpet of tiny yellow and blue flowers...but within two months everything green turned brown leaving little evidence that life existed."* This is why irrigation is essential to the farming success throughout the entire Great Central Valley during the dry summer months.

By 1872 an extension of the Central Pacific Railroad passed through the settlement of Merced paving the way for its growth. Railroad officials determined that this would be a good jumping-off point for tourists going to Yosemite Valley, so they sold the surrounding land to investors at high prices. That same year, a hotel named the Cosmopolitan was constructed to meet the needs of visitors; it had 175 rooms! Unfortunately, in 1929, the first year of the Great Depression, it burned down.

In 1874 a courthouse was built thus establishing Merced's permanence on the map. It is a museum today and a fine example of 19th century architecture. No gold strikes were ever made at this location, but agriculture has been equally as profitable. And just like other towns spanning the Central Valley, Merced helped supply the needs of miners in the foothills of the Sierra.

SNELLING & MERCED FALLS

It's hard to believe that the little town of Snelling was once home to thousands of people with Merced county's first courthouse (which is still there), several stores, a hotel, blacksmiths, four lawyers, two doctors and a teacher. Today the town's population is only a fraction of what it was, but Snelling happened to be at a good location on a route that supplied miners in the Southern Mother Lode. It prospered for that reason during the 1850s.

Just east of Snelling was another important small community named Merced Falls. It was here that sheep and cattle could cross the Merced River and a trading post flourished. Soon, due to the region's plentiful wheat crop, a flour mill was built using the Merced River to power the grinding wheels. The town thrived as a woolen mill and an iron **foundry** were promptly constructed. But the area was prone to disasters such as flooding, and in 1895 a fire nearly destroyed the entire community.

The town survived when a saw mill began operations in the early 1900s once again reviving local businesses. The Yosemite Valley Railroad supplied the mill with logs brought down from the Sierra as blades rotated 24 hours a day. Dredging in the region also took place; however, by the 1940s a shortage of trees, the failing railroad, and a declining dredging industry all contributed to the collapse of the ill-fated town; Snelling was also affected. Today, only the shells of Merced Falls' lumber buildings exist beside piles of dredge tailings, but Snelling still remains as a small farming and service community.

MARIPOSA

It was John Charles Frémont, the famed military explorer and politician, who invested $3000 to acquire a huge land grant called Las Mariposas. He obtained his 44,386 acres through the American Consul in Monterey when Mexico still ruled California. After the War with Mexico, gold was discovered, and Frémont floated his unestablished property lines to include some of the richest quartz mines in the southern mining district: eventually gaining a controversial but legal land title under U. S. law. A true Mother Lode town, Mariposa rapidly grew from a small settlement into a county seat that once covered 30,000 miles!

Frémont's mining operation temporarily made him a millionaire (on paper), but in the end he lost it all due to tremendous debts for costly hardrock equipment, legal battles, and outright scandals. By 1854 Mariposa had its own courthouse, where many mining laws were established, and a weekly newspaper—two of the oldest existing institutions in the state. Visit Mariposa's excellent museum and historic courthouse for a true flash of the mid 19th century past.

Mariposa, largest of California's original 27 counties—today there are 58.

MOUNT BULLION

This town was never very big, but the large sum of $3 million in gold was taken from its famous Princeton Mine. Hardrock mining machines smashed ore 24 hours a day, and it was said that a person on a horse in the late 1850s could ride to the thunderous pummel of stamp mills nonstop from here to Lake Tahoe!

MOUNT OPHIR

A myth that eight-sided $50 gold coins were privately minted here by assayer John L. Moffat in 1852 has been popular over the decades, but those coins were never struck at this location. The story was simply an attempt to create tourism in the area: promoted in part by a local newspaper. It did, however, encourage would-be treasure hunters who destroyed remaining historical buildings in their ruthless search for nonexistent gold throughout the years.

Mount Ophir was in truth host to a hardrock mine that was only moderately productive. Like many other towns that grew almost overnight and disappeared nearly as quickly when the gold was gone, Mount Ophir was able to quietly survive as a small supply center before becoming a complete ghost town. Only the ruins of a few shyly hidden slate stone walls entombed by a canopy of trees and thick underbrush remain.

BEAR VALLEY

In the early 1850s Bear Valley was populated by thousands. As part of the Mariposa land grant, this is where its most famous citizen John Frémont built one of his family homes so he could attend mining business, or appraise court proceedings in the neighboring town of Mariposa brought against him regarding exclusive mining rights. He actually spent little time here favoring his larger, luxurious San Francisco residence where the climate was more agreeable.

By 1865 Frémont's stake in the Mariposa was gone. His house, that was within eyeshot of the Bear Valley jail, fell into disrepair and burned in an 1866 fire. Where famous people, wealth, and miners' shacks once stood, only a small population remains.

The slate stone remains of the Bear Valley jail. When in use, a large iron eyelet embedded in the cell's concrete floor provided a secure hold for threading the chain of the prisoner's ankle cuffs making escape more difficult.

Self-Test: *MERCED TO BEAR VALLEY*

1. Describe the San Joaquin Valley before it was altered: _____
_____
_____
_____
_____

2. What was Snelling like before its decline? _____
_____
_____

3. Name three types of mills that operated in Merced Falls: _____
_____

    a.   What kind of disaster destroyed the town in 1895? _____
    b.   Why did Merced Falls lose its importance? _____
_____
_____

4. Name the type of mining that took place at Mount Bullion: _____

5. What town never produced $50 gold coins? _____

    a. Why was the rumor started? _____
_____

    b. What happened as a result of this rumor? _____
_____

6. Describe how large Mariposa County was at one time: _____
_____
_____

7. Briefly tell about John C. Frémont's life on his land grant: _____
_____
_____
_____
_____

HORNITOS

Very likely adopting its name from the Spanish word for "Little Ovens," it is a possible reference to the oven-shaped burial chambers that the Mexicans constructed above ground. That aside, Hornitos was one of the most heck-raising places in the Mother Lode. With a huge roving population by the early 1850s, this town supported four hotels, countless saloons and six supply stores that included Domingo Ghirardelli's: who later became famous making chocolate in San Francisco.

At one time thousands of dollars every month in rough gold was being shipped from here to San Francisco by Wells Fargo stagecoaches with heavily armed drivers. Today only the ruins of a single slate stone wall marks the existence of its collection office.

The settlement was also known for its lawlessness and vice. The town's Spanish-style plaza was once the scene of boundless gambling tables, festive dances, and brutal killings. It also claims in its history to be a haven for outlaws real and imagined.

The restless days of Hornitos are all but gone now, but it prevails as one of the few towns that gives visitors a hauntingly quiet but realistic sense of history from another time.

Remains of adobe wall in background reflects Mexican influence in Hornitos.

INDIAN GULCH

A town originally named Santa Cruz by Mexican miners who first settled here, little more than three buildings remain today in various conditions. But in its heyday there was canvas tent stores, saloons, gambling dens, a hotel, and blacksmith's shop. It was never the crossroads of superabundant gold strikes, and losing its importance, abandoned structures fell into disrepair. Before long, only the cemetery retained the name Santa Cruz as this out of the way place became known as Indian Gulch.

With time, the area became a refuge for horse and cattle thieves. Since stealing those animals took away a person's ability to make a living, the penalty was often death. Getting caught quickly abbreviated a thief's life with a tight rope around his neck and a short drop. Sometimes a murderer would be released if he had a defensible reason for killing another person, but rarely would there be a pardon for "horse thieving." The town was kept alive into the 1930s until its last store owner, Nicola Solari, passed away. Today a rancher's sheep graze in the solitude of this once ambitious establishment.

LA GRANGE

Settled by French miners in late 1849, placer gold rewarded them well, but when the easy gold was taken, a new way of mining was introduced: hydraulic. If you get a chance to visit La Grange, look at the surrounding landscape. It appears that the hillsides in the area are eroding naturally. To a point this is correct, but water cannons have also assisted in leaving their scars when miners blasted the ancient uplifted riverbed sediments above the Tuolumne River gorge—exposing the precious gold they sought.

La Grange is also associated with at least one famous person you may have heard about—Bret Harte. He allegedly taught school here for a short time, but that never happened. He was, however, employed as a Wells Fargo Express gun guard for a short period in the late 1850s, thus familiar with the mines, miners, and many colorful towns of the day. Fame did come his way later in life when he wrote about the Gold Rush in the spirit of the people who lived it. One such popular story is titled: *The Outcasts of Poker Flat*.

In 1917 large-scale dredging was established in this vicinity. Just outside town you can still see what is left of one called the Tuolumne Dredge or "Grey Goose." Regrettably, it was scrapped in the 1980s, and little more than the ruins of a rusty, nondescript boxy frame remains. When in use, the 3000 ton electrically powered monolith worked the ground of this area digging its own pond as it washed out countless tons of gold-bearing river gravels. This machine went out of service in the early 1940s, but the huge piles of tailings it left behind are enduring signs of its presence.

COULTERVILLE

At the time gold was discovered, this Mexican dominated camp quickly burst into a tent town that wandering prospectors and merchants found especially prosperous. Miners of several nationalities populated the area including many Chinese who were lured by rich placer streams. The village had other names in its past, but it was George W. Coulter's blue canvas supply tent that became a well-known landmark in 1850. The settlement eventually adopted Coulter's name because of his notable recognition. Fires burned main street to the ground three times over the years, but the town always rebounded because hardrock mining continued to bring the region prosperity well into the 1900s.

Getting ore from the hillside mines to the stamp mills was always an ever present challenge, but the difficulty was solved in part by machine technology when the Merced Mining Company purchased a small steam engine in 1897. Built in Pittsburgh, Pennsylvania it was transported around the Horn of South America to San Francisco where It was carried in sections by mule train to Coulterville. There it was put to work hauling ore from steep mountainside mines to the mills puffing along on narrow gauge iron tracks. That same engine, named "Whistling Billy," is currently on display outside the historical museum next to Highway 49.

In its long past, Coulterville served as a popular stopover for travelers enroute to Yosemite Valley until more direct roads guided them away. The town is important today because it is an historical landmark where slate stone walls of former buildings are intact and the original Chinese Sun Sun Wo store built of adobe brick in 1851 still stands.

The Whistling Billy on display along Highway 49 in Coulterville.

65

CHINESE CAMP

The Chinese were probably the most persecuted ethnic group in the Mother Lode. Their society, language and dress was so different from the overwhelming majority of other cultures, they could be easily singled out by the intolerant few.

Chinese mining companies who settled in this area generally escaped abuse, and they also found valuable gold deposits, often by reworking what other miners thought was worthless. By 1856 Chinese Camp was on part of a major freight route, and had a population numbering in the low thousands. However, this was also when the

Chinese built stone fences span miles of foothills in the gold country.

town's two major "tongs" (secret Chinese societies) began quarreling. The argument was probably over a mining issue, but whatever the reason, hundreds of men on each side had local blacksmiths making a variety of spears and knives for the event that was about to emerge.

On September 26, the warriors met in an open field prepared to settle their dispute. The clash took place, but to the surprise of the many onlookers who came to witness the contest, it turned out to be mostly a show of strength, and loud, angry voices instead of an all-out battle. In the end only one man had been accidentally stabbed and died, and one was wounded. It was remembered as the Tong or Crimea War since it was held across from the Crimea Ranch near Chinese Camp. Today modern street signs have been placed next to the old stone posts that marked main crossings of this once active foothill village.

SONORA

Taking its name from miners who came up from Sonora, Mexico, it was also known as the "Queen of the Mother Lode" since it was one of the richest settlements in the area. Millions of dollars in golden treasure would eventually be taken in all. One memorable nugget weighed in at 25 pounds! This Latin-influenced community became a dangerous place to live when Americans felt that the gold on United States soil should not be a free-for-all, and noncitizens should be forbidden to possess claims. The resulting dispute led to a conflict where rough sets of foreigners and American citizens fought, raided and occasionally murdered each other. Most everyone wore a gun, and isolated camps as well as the streets of Sonora were no longer safe, especially at night.

In 1850 the California Legislature passed a law billed the Foreign Miners' Tax to raise money for the new state and in part to encourage citizenship. This law required that all noncitizens pay a $20 fee every month in order to work their claims. The law was no doubt unpopular among the many foreign miners who were already here, and a number departed or ventured to more remote areas to avoid it. Merchants disliked it as well because they suffered a loss of business as a result. The tax was cancelled a year later, but it was shortly reintroduced at a lesser fee of $3 per month.

Sonora's natural gold reserves eventually diminished, but since the town was located on a route to Stockton, a major supply center, it remained an important transportation link to other mining camps. Today, Sonora continues to thrive as tourists come to visit the lasting reminders of a livelier time.

Self-Test: *HORNITOS TO SONORA*

1.   How did Hornitos get its name? _____
_____

     a.   What made Ghirardelli famous in San Francisco? _____

     b.   At its peak, how much gold was taken a month from Hornitos? _____

2.   Why was the penalty for stealing a horse often worse than killing another person?
_____
_____

3.   How did Bret Harte become famous?_____

     a.   What was the "Grey Goose?" _____

4.   Describe how the "Whistling Billy" got to Coulterville and its purpose: _____
_____
_____
_____
_____

5.   Why were the Chinese persecuted? _____
_____

     a.   What is a tong? _____

6.   What was the purpose of the Foreign Miners' Tax? _____
_____
_____

     a.   Explain why you think the tax was fair or unfair:_____
_____
_____

     b.   Why did Sonora remain an important town after the gold was gone? _____
_____

COLUMBIA

This camp is typical of what sparked a boomtown. Thaddeus and George Hildreth with their party happened to wander here after a period of bad luck searching for gold elsewhere. Seeing Mexican miners already finding gold in the area, John Walker, another man with the brothers, did a little panning himself to see how he would do. The date was March 27, 1850. In the two days that followed, the men gathered nearly thirty pounds of nuggets! Soon word spread of the new strike, and the group of tents that became part of the scenery was known as "Hildreth Diggin's." But like many other original places, it was not uncommon for a name to change. The settlement was also known as American Camp for a short time, and then finally evolved permanently into Columbia—all in the same year.

It wasn't long until miners discovered they were on top of an ancient stream bed of the Stanislaus River that had long since changed course. The few creeks that drained through the area dried up during the summer months, so two water companies developed a system of ditches and a 60 mile long flume that supplied water to power mining machinery. In a snap, hydraulic and hardrock mining equipment was brought in and put to work extracting gold at a record rate.

Columbia quickly became one of California's largest settlements. The town included four banks, eight hotels, two fire stations, three churches, a school, 53 general stores, and the usual entertainment facilities that boasted three theaters, countless saloons, and gambling places to satisfy most any need or want. Unfortunately an 1854 fire burned down most every building in the business district since many structures were wood. The town was rebuilt and the new stores were constructed chiefly of brick or stone with swinging metal door and window coverings for security, and to minimize future fire destruction.

By the 1870s about $87 million in gold had been taken from Columbia; today that amount in our dollars would top $2 billion. But just like other towns that finally gave up most of their gold, Columbia also became a ghost town. However, in 1945 the State of California bought the land and many of the old buildings and created a "Living" State Historical Park where men and women dress and play the roles of Gold Rush era personalities.

Columbia is one of the most popular Mother Lode towns where more than half a million people visit each year to witness reenactments and participate in a multitude of hands-on activities of another century.

Wells Fargo stage station in Columbia. Most famous of all carriers, serving banking, security, delivery and passenger needs throughout the state.

CARSON HILL

In 1850, miners struck gold here. In 1851, a 14 pound nugget was dug up. Three years later the largest mass of gold ever found in California was unearthed weighing in at 195 pounds! Mixed in quartz it was four feet long, two feet wide and five inches thick. At the time this lump was worth $43,500 at $16 an ounce. Overall, about $25 million was taken from the hill, and mining continues sporadically to this day.

In the early days, high-grade gold ore was painstakingly chiseled out of deep candle lit mine shafts by men using hand tools. Then a short iron cart called a "skip" was filled with about half a ton of the precious cargo. At this point the cart was pulled to the surface by a mule along thin metal tracks to the stamps. But unlike mines of yesteryear, tunnels on the most part are relics of the past.

Technology has made it possible to excavate entire mountains resulting in massive open pits. Large-scale operations today use powerful machines to shovel rocky blocks of ore into huge dump trucks that sit on wheels eight feet tall! Each moves about like an obedient mechanical dinosaur hauling nearly 100 tons of ore to the mill in one trip! Still, a majority of gold taken from contemporary mines is microscopic, so incredible amounts of ore must be processed in order to profit, and the gold must be chemically removed.

Ore carts or "skips" were once pulled by mules.

Giant Lectra Haul dump truck taking ore to the mill.

MARK TWAIN'S CABIN

The man who wrote *The Adventures of Tom Sawyer and Huckleberry Finn* caught gold fever himself, and came west in 1861 by stagecoach. He tried prospecting, but mainly supported his aloof life-style by working as a reporter. Although he never struck it rich during his wanderings throughout Nevada and California, he did find the inspiration in the Mother Lode to write: *The Celebrated Jumping Frog of Calaveras County*, a very popular tale.

The original cabin he rented just outside of Angels Camp burned to the ground some years after he left, but it was eventually rebuilt around the original fireplace and chimney. If you use your imagination, one can almost see Twain,

Protected remains where Mark Twain lived for a short time.

whose real name was Samuel Clemens, sitting inside his small cabin behind a table, watching a crackling fire on a cold winter morning, sipping coffee, and writing notes for stories. Twain lived here during 1864-65: the final two years of the Civil War.

ANGELS CAMP

George Angel was part of a group that discovered placer gold on this spot, but Angel found that he could do better selling goods and soon made a fortune supplying miners. For example, when demand was high, a $3 red flannel shirt might go for $15 and a common shovel could reach tenfold its normal amount. These prices would have been outrageous in the eastern states, but no one complained too much because most miners were finding enough gold by 1850 to keep a stock of provisions which discouraged them from going to get cheaper supplies elsewhere. Besides, leaving a claim would cost time and a chance to hit it big—it *could* happen, and at any moment.

Angels Camp was complete with a Wells Fargo Express station and ever present assayer who bought rough gold directly from the miners, melted it down into heavy bars, then had them transported to San Francisco with armed guards. From there the gold was shipped by sea to eastern banks to create currency and finance loans. Inevitably, the large deposits of local placer gold became exhausted on the most part. Angels Camp might have become a ghost town, but a new discovery led to another type of mining which kept Angels Camp alive for many more decades—treasure in the form of gold-bearing ore.

Ore is simply a mineral mixed within rock. Ore in the Mother Lode is typically gold formed within a milky white, glass-like rock called quartz. Gold-bearing quartz found protruding from the ground is known as an outcrop. However, the sources of these outcroppings plunge deep into the earth and had to be followed by miners. Tunnels were created as miners broke up the ore into smaller pieces where it was sent to be crushed and the gold extracted. The gold contained within the quartz varied from microscopic particles to visible lines or "veins" within the rock which helped determine the value and practicability of processing the ore. Still there was no guarantee a profit would be made over the long run and many a miner lost everything he was worth as he picked, blasted, hauled and crushed ore that became nearly worthless as the expenses of specialized machinery increased and rewards decreased. This was rarely the case in Angels Camp. Companies that engaged in hardrock mining here added profits totaling in the millions.

As a result of this type of mining, approximately 40,000 mine shafts have been excavated throughout the Sierran gold country speckling the entire length of the Mother Lode from Mariposa to Downieville. Some still remain active to this day. Large-scale hardrock mining is all but a memory in Angels Camp now, but reminders abound everywhere. The local museum and park dedicated to the miners of the productive Utica Mine are first rate. The town still celebrates the Gold Rush each May and includes a frog jumping contest made popular by a story credited to Mark Twain who spent time here during his travels. A statue of him also stands in the park commemorating a movie made about him in the 1970s.

Hardrock miners in 1882.
Courtesy Levi Strauss & Co., San Francisco

70

MURPHYS

John and Daniel Murphy were camped here in 1848 when they struck it rich panning $400 in one day! The brothers got along well with the local Indians who were happy to trade the gold they found for what they considered more practical items such as blankets and foods. Within a year the Murphy brothers left, but it should be known that these men were different from most miners: they both left rich, and the prosperity continued.

Wells Fargo and Company was quick to build a carrier station as they did in most every boomtown. The glut of raw gold in settlements like this caused the price of the metal to drop; therefore, it could be purchased at a significantly lower price and later resold at a higher one. In addition, Wells Fargo's network of stages transported passengers, freight, and mail throughout California, and, of course, gold. The company hauled out no less than $15 million from this choice area to its home base in San Francisco.

The town flourished and many buildings were constructed over the years, including a bowling alley. One of the more famous structures that remains is the Murphys Hotel built in 1856. It continues to accommodate visitors today as it did when dusty travelers stepped down from stagecoaches.

Murphys Hotel still stands as a proud icon of the Gold Rush, and modern day visitors can still stay the night.

STOCKTON

Stockton gained its importance by being situated next to the San Joaquin River which was deep enough for steamships to connect it with San Francisco. Named after the popular naval war hero Robert Stockton, it was a main supply artery and starting point for miners and merchants alike in the southern mining district. One important land route from here connected Sonora in the foothills to the east, and another, the Miller-Stockton road, led all the way to the far-reaching military outpost Fort Miller over 150 miles south; parts of the trail can still be seen today. Many traveled to and from this busy San Joaquin Valley town, and it remains an active recreational and transportation center today.

Self-Test: COLUMBIA TO STOCKTON

1. Briefly summarize Columbia's history from 1850 to the present: _____

_____

_____

_____

_____

_____

   a. Why were buildings made from brick with metal doors and window coverings?

   _____

   _____

   _____

   b. Explain what had to be done before hydraulic mining could take place:

   _____

   _____

   _____

   c. By the 1870s how much gold had been taken from Columbia? _____

2. Describe the largest single mass of gold ever taken during the Gold Rush: _____

   _____

   _____

3. Contrast hardrock mining in its early days to similar mines today: _____

   _____

   _____

   _____

   _____

4. Name two books Mark Twain (Samuel Clemens) wrote: _____

   _____

Continued...

SUPPLIES PURCHASED IN ANGELS CAMP:

(Items and prices taken from actual 1850 account. Prices varied greatly due to availability of goods—supply and demand)

TOOLS

1 cradle	$18.00
1 pan	2.00
1 dipper	1.25
1 bucket	1.00
2 picks	10.50
1 shovel	11.00

TOTAL$

FOOD

25 lbs. flour	$5.00
9 lbs. pork	2.70
4 lbs. beef	1.20
1 jar pickles	8.00
1 pint molasses	.50
2 lbs. sugar	.60
Ground coffee	5.00
2 lbs. potatoes	.25

TOTAL$

OTHER

1 pair boots	$10.00
2 shirts	5.00
Pants	8.25
2 blankets	10.00
Canvas tent	30.00
2 candles	.50
1 mule	65.00

TOTAL$

5. Hardrock mining kept Angels Camp productive for decades. What is meant by hardrock mining?

_____

_____

_____

_____

a. Why did miners sometimes have to pay high prices for the things they needed?

_____

_____

6. Why did Wells Fargo and Company build a station in nearly every rich boomtown?_____

_____

_____

_____

7. What else made Murphys a one of a kind town other than gold? _____

_____

_____

8. Why did many paths lead to Stockton? _____

_____

_____

_____

_____

MOKELUMNE HILL

Rating as another of the wildest camps in the Mother Lode, this community is situated on the rising knolls above the river from which it shares its name. Mokelumne Hill was originally founded by Jonathan Stevenson, an ex-Colonel of the Mexican War turned goldseeker. In 1851, several other major gold strikes were made, and the entire region rapidly grew.

Two of the larger ethnic groups who settled here were the French, and Chileans of South America. But with claims staked closely together, it wasn't long before tensions over mining rights spurred fights that occurred in the saloons that stayed open all hours. Brawls were commonplace, and even murders were the hard reality of this town's early history.

Before long, the easiest found gold ran out as always; new strikes were made elsewhere, and Mokelumne Hill, once populated by thousands, nearly disappeared by the 1860s.

Iron window and door coverings reduced fire hazard and theft.

VOLCANO

Established in 1848, Volcano was so named because inquiring prospectors thought that an ancient volcano had exploded, and the existing valley was its crater. That was a good assumption, but unknown to miners of the time, it was really the eroded bend of an extinct riverbed which happened to be loaded with rich deposits of gold. Pans, rockers, and sluice boxes skimmed off the cream, then the explosive blasts of hydraulic cannons soon followed proving to be the best method for effectively taking a majority of the fortune.

Another inspiring detail about Volcano is that its early residents seemed to be committed to exercising their minds as well as the gold fields challenged their bodies. They very well may have organized the state's first lending library, theatre group, and debating society. Nevertheless, the town went dormant as the gold was depleted, but the shells of many old structures remain standing in this geologically christened town.

Hand-cut blocks of stone built this Mokelumne Hill store.

"L. Mayer & Son 1854, GAGE Build'r"

74

JACKSON

One of the four original Kennedy Tailings Wheels.   F. P. A. Photo

First referred to as "Botilleas" by Mexican settlers, it was a popular natural spring where travelers could fill their water bottles. It was later renamed Jackson, very likely in honor of Andrew Jackson, our seventh President.

Gold had been found earlier, but in 1856 Andrew Kennedy discovered a rich quartz vein that would make his name famous. The area was exceptionally productive and various hardrock mining operations took place here until 1942. The yield of Jackson's two most famous mines, the Kennedy and Argonaut, totaled $34 million—the length of one of

Kennedy Wheel #4: Rotating right to left, chambers on the outer ring scooped up waste tailings channeled to it by a flume. As the wheel turned, gravity caused the thick, runny sludge to fall out on the left side to another flume where it was relayed to the next wheel and finally containment dam. Completed by 1914, there were four in all—two remain today.

these tunnels sloped into the ground following an ore vein nearly 6000 feet; that's more than a mile!

Jackson has other unique locations worth investigating too, such as the Kennedy Wheels. Built of wood with metal supports and resembling Ferris wheels, four were constructed to scoop up and elevate runny mud-like tailings to a holding dam 128 feet uphill from where the gold processing took place. Because a poisonous chemical was used in the **cyanide process** to dissolve gold from crushed ore, these hazardous tailings became a public safety concern. Loosely controlled, widespread use of toxins used by miners led the government to pass laws as early as 1912. The new rulings forced mining companies to contain their tailings which helped deter groundwater contamination: this is why the wheels near Jackson were built. Only two survive relatively intact today, but they are very impressive to see as each stands 58 feet tall.

SUTTER CREEK

Named after John Sutter, hardrock mining put this town on the map. Placer gold was never very plentiful, but in the surrounding area, which is Amador County today, several deep mine shafts produced ore that totaled millions of dollars. The streets are still lined with many brick buildings of the late 1800s that show off the wealth of the past.

Another lasting feature of the town not to be overlooked is its water-powered iron works. Established in 1873, the Knight Foundry made fittings used to hold together tunnel supports and parts and equipment required for hardrock mines in the area. They still cast specialty items today using methods that have changed very little over time.

Items cast at the Kennedy Foundry.

AMADOR CITY

Phenomenal wealth didn't start with the tent city of goldseekers who sought the rich placers that generously speckled nearby creeks. But it did prominently emerge when a nearby quartz vein was discovered by a Baptist minister in 1851. Lode gold abounded in Amador, and hardrock miners fed rich ore to bustling stamp mills that would extract the treasure day and night for decades.

In the 1860s the Keystone Mine became its most famous gold producer. At its peak $40,000 a month was taken from the abundantly rich quartz for a total of over $24 million. Production continued until 1942 when the mine permanently closed.

The headquarters where Keystone's miners once collected their paychecks has been remodeled as a museum and contains many relics of the past. Also, the rusted **headframe** that lowered and raised workers, equipment and ore carts into the mine shaft still exists marking this tunnel's place in history.

Headframes supported equipment that lowered and raised miners and ore from deep inside the earth.

Skeletal headframe over abandoned Fremont Mine near Amador City.

FIDDLETOWN

Old miners were always complaining that the younger ones were *"fiddlin' around"* all the time, thus the name Fiddletown. True or not, placer gold was first panned here in 1849 and settled by people from the state of Missouri. Stamp mills were churning ore by the mid 1850s, and hydraulic monitors splashed away in the countryside less than ten years later.

Several thousand called this place home—including a large Chinese population. In fact, one of the most interesting buildings that remains is the Chew Kee Store which is built of **rammed earth**. At one time Chinese residents bought everything here from specialty foods to herbal remedies to cure illnesses.

Few people live here today, but it remains one of the rare places that projects a Gold Rush era feeling of wonder.

Chew Kee Store with walls built of rammed earth.

Self-Test: MOKELUMNE HILL TO FIDDLETOWN

1. Name two large ethnic groups who settled in Mokelumne Hill: _____
   _____

   a. What was one reason fights took place? _____
      _____

2. Why did miners give Volcano its name, and was it accurate? _____
   _____
   _____

   a. How did residents exercise their minds as well as the gold fields challenged their bodies?
      _____
      _____

3. What was Jackson's original name, and why was it named this? _____
   _____

   a. Name the two mines where $34 million was taken: _____

   b. Describe why the four Kennedy Wheels were built: _____
      _____
      _____
      _____

4. Why do many of Sutter Creek's buildings remain? _____
   _____

   a. Why was the Knight Foundry important to hardrock miners? _____
      _____

5. What was the purpose of the headframe in Amador City's Keystone mine? _____
   _____

6. Name three mining methods used in Fiddletown: _____
   _____

   a. Summarize how a rammed earth wall is made: _____
      _____
      _____
      _____
      _____

PLACERVILLE

"Dry Diggings," the first of more familiar names to come, was known so because its creeks were often waterless during summer. It was soon more colorfully changed to Hangtown because people there got fed up with law breakers. A person could be accused, tried, convicted and dangling with a noose around his neck in about two hours—and it happened—when found guilty by a **vigilante justice** committee.

As with other early boomtowns, gold was plentiful in the surrounding area and there were many places one could part with his money. By 1854 this mining village possessed several hotels, a theatre, church, and numerous restaurants, saloons and gambling halls. As the town developed into a busy trans-Sierran link, its citizens decided to switch its name again to make it sound more inviting to passing visitors. It was renamed Placerville with respect to the large amount of placer gold found here and has remained so ever since. And like most towns rapidly constructed of wood and canvas, Placerville too was plagued by fire: nearly burning to the ground in 1856, it was fast built again with brick and stone.

In its long history many changes have shaped this settlement that traditionally marks the boundary of the northern and southern mining districts, including transportation and communication technologies. Stagecoaches once passed this way when a suitable trail through the Sierra was opened, and a telegraph line was set up even before Pony Express riders carried news and mail on their way to and from Sacramento. The Central Pacific Railroad laid track in this lively town as well. Today that same route is Highway 50 which is a major road to Lake Tahoe, a popular resort area. Placerville is still a successful community not because of gold, but its location.

Placerville circa 1854, notice sluice box in foreground and Methodist Episcopal Church in back. Kansas State Historical Society

Cook a famous breakfast, The Hangtown Fry:

1/2 pound bacon
6 to 10 oysters
6 eggs
Crush a handful of plain crackers

1/4 cup heavy cream
1/4 cup parmesan cheese (grated)

Fry bacon crisp and set aside. Remove most of the grease from skillet. Dip oysters in 2 beaten eggs, then roll oysters in cracker crumbs. Fry in bacon grease over medium heat, about one minute per side. Beat 4 more eggs with cream, cheese and add anything else you have available that might taste good (that's what they did!). Season with salt and pepper to suit your taste. Pour mixture over oysters in skillet, reduce heat scrambling eggs until cooked. Serves 2 or 3.

COLOMA

It all began here with an unlikely but providential relationship. Two men, John Augustus Sutter, and James Wilson Marshall, set into motion a chain of events that caused the world to rush for California's gold.

Originally from Switzerland, Sutter left his homeland to escape debtor's prison, and in the process his family who would not reunite with him for many years. Mexico still controlled California when Sutter entered by way of Hawaii, and upon his arrival in 1839, convinced government officials in Monterey that he was a war hero, and they should let him establish a settlement. The governor agreed, and Sutter, who became a Mexican citizen, had a rectangular adobe brick fortification built on a site near the convergence of the American and Sacramento Rivers with the help of Indian labor. He named his land grant New Helvetia (New Switzerland), and his upstart trading post became known as Sutter's Fort.

Nearly a decade passed, and Sutter, needing more lumber for his growing demands, hired a carpenter who came from New Jersey by the name of James Marshall. It was agreed he would design and build a water-powered saw mill on the south fork of the American River some 40 miles away where trees abounded in a valley known as Coloma. Construction began, and while inspecting the **tailrace** that was nearly completed, Marshall noticed something shine in the water.

The year was 1848, most likely the morning of January 24. In the days that followed, Marshall

Marshall Monument, located at Gold Discovery State Park, Coloma.

journeyed to the trade fort and curiously delivered to Sutter what he thought was gold. They tested the pea-sized nuggets, confirmed it was the mineral, then swore secrecy which, of course, didn't last.

The small pieces of gold Marshall found on that morning might have been worth only a few dollars, but little did he know that when word got out, and it did almost immediately, he would be credited for introducing the world's best-known gold rush—the California Gold Rush!

Almost overnight Coloma became a boomtown. In less than a year the settlement had 13 hotels, two banks, countless stores and saloons, tents everywhere, hundreds of claims, outrageous prices for everything and a population of several thousand who spent their earnings freely. Soon other strikes were discovered throughout the region, and the rush was really on.

Unfortunately for Sutter and Marshall, they never struck it rich. Sutter could not control the flood of people who invaded and took over his property. His fort fell into disorder, and he sold it in the fall of 1849. Fed up with California, he eventually relocated to a Swiss community in Pennsylvania where he spent the last two years of his life trying to recover his perceived financial losses from Congress. Sutter died in 1880 while in Washington D.C.

Marshall's end was even more tragic. He never found much gold, so he tried his luck in business, then wine making, and failed in both. Finally he went back to what he knew best—the skill of repairing things. He was drinking heavily late in life and eventually ended up in a small town several miles southeast of Coloma named Kelsey. There he operated a carpenter and blacksmith shop. This is where he also confirmed his reputation as an exaggerator (he claimed to have mystical powers for finding gold), and was sadly a semi-reclusive alcoholic who would sell autographed "Gold Discovery Cards" for a few cents. He died in 1885 the wreckage of his own disappointments.

Upon his death the citizens of Kelsey did not know what to do with Marshall's body since he had no immediate family nearby. Due to the summer heat, they put him in a wagon filled with ice and took him to Coloma. His corpse would lay five days before it was finally decided to bury him on top of a hill that overlooked the valley where he had found gold many years earlier.

By 1890, a group known as the Native Sons helped immortalize the significance of Marshall's discovery by convincing the California Legislature to set aside funds to commission a monument honoring him. The nine foot statue dedicated above Marshall's grave stands on top a tall concrete foundation but is not made of bronze as it appears. Rather, it's a mixture of lead, tin and zinc coated with a bronze-like color to look expensive. The figure shows the larger than life Marshall pointing to the river that made him famous but failed to make him rich. In his right hand he grasps a huge nugget (he never found) as a token of his importance. Marshall may or may not have been a great man in life, but he now stands as a well-known icon that reminds us of an important historical era.

Today Coloma is a 220 acre state park with many interesting sights to see. It includes a replica of the saw mill that was built in 1968, but it is not on the original spot. After only a few years of service the first mill was dismantled for various uses and floods all but erased its presence by 1857. In 1924 archaeologists established its exact location, and a stone marker was erected. Some of the **artifacts** unearthed at the site are on display at the park's quality museum. A person could spend a whole day exploring Coloma, and a worthwhile visit is recommended.

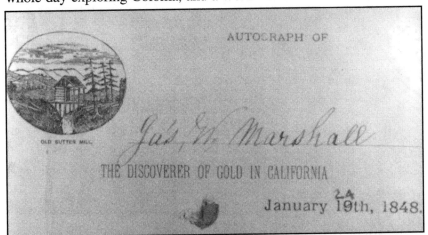

"Gold Discovery Card"
It appears that even Marshall was never quite sure of the actual date he first found gold when these cards were printed. But a crudely written diary by one of the Mormon laborers who helped build the saw mill provided evidence for the most likely date of discovery, and Marshall must have been aware of this.
California State Library Archive

AUBURN

Placer gold abounded here in 1848, and it was not unheard of for a man to pan a small fortune in a day. But... you guessed it, the gold ran out. Auburn might have become a ghost town except that its location made it an important trading center.

Many stagecoaches came this way, and the first recorded robbery of one took place here. The future of the town was assured when Central Pacific Railroad officials decided to lay track through Auburn on their way to Utah.

Today houses and businesses in the old section of the city are built on the same hilly streets that miners walked more than 150 years ago.

Self-Test: PLACERVILLE TO NEVADA CITY

1. Describe how all three of Placerville's names came about: _____

_____

_____

_____

_____

_____

    a. What destroyed the town in 1856? _____

    b. Name all of the changes in communication and transportation this town has

        seen in its early history: _____

        _____

        _____

        _____

        _____

        _____

        _____

2. What country controlled California when John Sutter arrived? _____

    a. Write a summary for John Sutter and his role in the California Gold Rush:

    _____

_____

_____

_____

_____

_____

_____

_____

_____

_____

_____

Continued...

Self-Test: PLACERVILLE TO NEVADA CITY

b. Write a summary for James Marshall and his role in the Gold Rush:

_____

_____

_____

_____

_____

_____

_____

_____

_____

_____

c. Explain why you believe Marshall was or was not a famous person in your opinion:

_____

_____

_____

_____

3.   What crime had its beginnings in Auburn? _____

4.   Provide at least three reasons why Sacramento was an important city during the Gold Rush:

_____

a. What natural disaster was a problem for Sacramento in its early days? _____

_____

5.   Why did people first settle in Grass Valley? _____

a. Name the two largest hardrock mines in the area and the total amount of gold taken
   from them: _____

_____

6.   What mining method was invented near Nevada City? _____

MALAKOFF DIGGINGS & MARYSVILLE

It almost looks like the surface of another planet. Yet in the distance, tall pine trees loom above the rim of a large crater that reaches a depth of 600 feet, a mile and a half long, and is over half a mile wide.

Where are you? Northern California's Malakoff Diggings near the ghost town of North Bloomfield.

Hydraulic mining reached its high point in this area, and the heavily financed operation at Malakoff was especially productive. For instance, all the bits of gold collected in

Lamps on stands in right background lit the night. California State Library Archive

just one month during 1882 were melted down into a block that weighed 510 pounds! Seven powerful monitors pounded the surrounding hillsides from the bottom of this depression, and the largest one could discharge a million gallons of water an hour against the hard-packed sediments it shattered. The operation was relentless as miners stayed on the job around the clock working in continuous eight hour shifts.

Monitors or "giants" ripping away the hidden treasure in ancient riverbed gravels.
California State Library Archive

But this method of gold extraction was destructive in many indirect ways. The titanic proportions of heavy choking silt jettisoned from Malakoff's exit flume spilled into the bottom of the Yuba River and reached far beyond. Thus began a long chain-reaction that stretched to the conjunction of the Feather where the thriving town of Marysville sat: a farming, supply, and business center for the northern mining district—and it didn't stop there. Debris propelled by those two rivers entered the Pacific-bound Sacramento where the glutinous

muddy sludge washed into San Francisco Bay—over 160 miles distant—staining it brown! Mountain snowmelt during the spring compounded the problem ever more as it plunged down muck-filled river channels. The swell of fresh water, having no other place to go, resulted in widespread flooding that ruined farmers' fields and drenched the busy streets of Marysville three feet deep.

Finally in 1884, a California judge handed down America's first environmental judgment: mining companies could not dump their tailings into major rivers or their tributaries. Malakoff Diggings soon shut down, and the town of North Bloomfield that supplied the men working there was abandoned. Both are museums today, a tribute to the world's largest hydraulic mining enterprise.

OROVILLE

Located near the Feather River where it flows onto the San Joaquin Valley, this is where the first successful bucket-line dredge was used in 1898 to scoop up tons of sand and gravel to extract gold from a river bed. Some of the largest dredges in the state operated here, and the uniform piles of gravel that are common along the highways of this area indicate their work. They were big business, profitable, and operated for more than 60 years before the last one shut down.

Oroville is also remembered because of the possibility that the last remaining "wild" California native came here from his mountain home in 1911. He was hungry, confused, and alone. Everything he had once known had been either destroyed or taken. He was called Ishi, which means "man" in Yahi, the tribe he is believed to have come from. Read *Ishi: Last of His Tribe* by Theodora Krober to learn more.

DOWNIEVILLE & SIERRAVILLE

It was a difficult trail and nearly 3000 feet of elevation that made Downieville less accessible than most other camps, but that didn't keep miners away from the rich placer deposits found in and around the north fork of the Yuba River. This settlement enjoyed many prosperous years before fading, but it was another event that made this town somewhat more famous than gold.

Although the facts are not perfectly clear, around 1851, a miner got into an argument with a woman. He apparently kicked in her door, and at some point during their disagreement she stabbed and killed him. The murdered man was the friend of many miners, and an angry group of vigilantes quickly determined her fate—to hang at the end of a rope. She was the first woman executed in California.

Extending to its most northern reach, the Mother Lode completely fizzles out near the town of Sierraville. Here the gold country quietly dissolves where a picturesque valley bordered by the jagged snowy peaks of the Sierra high country meet. Here too, goldseekers swarmed with the hope that the next mountain or stream held the fortune they came so far to shout, *"Eureka!"* (I have found it).

Yet for an overwhelming majority, the quest for wealth eluded them. After months of wandering from tent camp to boomtown, thoughts of ending their search began to linger. Since most found only enough gold to live by hand and mouth and survived in conditions less than comfortable, they looked for other opportunities and became the developers of early California. Many others simply decided that the best of all possible worlds was the place where their dreams and long journey had begun—home.

CONCLUSION:

There are many other interesting Gold Rush towns and locations, but the selection briefly covered is very representative of the conditions, events and personalities of this era. California was a magnet for the determined crush of gold-hunters who came in force. And even though other rich strikes in Nevada, Colorado, Montana, South Dakota and Alaska were discovered over the years, no other gold rush in the world would ever match the fury of California's. But even when the easiest gold had been removed, other kinds of economic wealth remained in the state. Agriculture and the timber industries as well as tourism among many others would keep California's economy booming as they do today. It is California's abundant resources, attractive climate, beautiful landscapes and the ambition of many varying ethnic backgrounds that have shaped the Golden State's future.

Nearly all of the towns that came to exist throughout and beyond the beltway of the Mother Lode were staked out because of gold, and along with the arrival of a new population came many ideas and changes both good and bad. On one hand this era saw the rise of transportation, communication and energy technologies that have affected our modern world for the better. On the other, the Indians' way of life was forever altered, and the exploitation or wholesale destruction and misuse of California's resources has damaged its condition. Although the people, land and towns of the Gold Rush have changed as the decades passed, many artifacts symbolizing the period have not. Today we can explore the distinctive history of generations before us when we walk among the ruins, buildings, and museums mirroring that past. For those who long to see a bygone century, we have the means to experience a time that helps us understand and keep our own values and destinations in focus.

Self-Test: MALAKOFF DIGGINGS TO DOWNIEVILLE

1. Describe the hydraulic mining pit at Malakoff: _____

    _____

    _____

    a. How many pounds did the largest block of gold taken at Malakoff weigh? _____

    b. How long were the shifts miners worked in this operation? _____

    _____

    c. How many gallons of water could the largest monitor discharge in one hour?

    _____

    d. What town was flooded as a result of hydraulic mining? _____

    e. This town supplied the miners at Malakoff Diggings: _____

2. Name the mining method that developed near Oroville: _____

    a. Who was Ishi? _____

    _____

3. What "first" is Downieville known for? _____

    _____

    a. Name the last town in the northern Sierra where the Mother Lode ends:_____

4. Interpret how California has progressed economically from the end of the Gold Rush until now:

    _____

    _____

    _____

    _____

    _____

    _____

    _____

    _____

Continued...

Self-Test: MALAKOFF DIGGINGS TO DOWNIEVILLE

5. Looking back on all of the towns you read about, describe the kinds of changes that took place in California during the Gold Rush era, and how they improved the quality of life:

6. Why are historical Gold Rush towns worth preserving?

1842   **Gold is discovered north of Los Angeles by ranch hand Francisco Lopez while in search of horses, but has no far-reaching influence.**

1848   James Marshall discovers gold on the American River triggering a major rush.

1849   **Hardrock mining begins at Mariposa. The first stamp mill in the state was probably used here.**

1850   Gold ore is found in Grass Valley. This leads to the development of an underground mining operation that lasts for over 100 years.

1852   **Hydraulic mining begins at American Hill just north of Nevada City.**

1854   A 195 pound mass of gold, the largest known during the rush, is found at Carson Hill. The "Gold Rush" technically ends as yearly gold production decreases from this point on. But the influence of California gold continues into the 20th century in some form.

1855   **The bulk of easy placer gold is largely exhausted by this date, but other methods of mining requiring machinery takes over.**

1857   The side-wheel steamship *Central America* sinks in a storm off the coast of South Carolina taking with it many lives and tons of California gold headed for New York banks.

1864   **Hardrock and hydraulic mining take over as the chief gold production methods. Other rich mineral strikes are still being made.**

1880   Hydraulic mining reaches its peak in the state. The same systems of reservoirs, tunnels, canals and flumes used to supply the water to monitors will also irrigate farmer's fields and power electrical generators as they become available providing a new and inexpensive source of energy.

1884   **Judge Lorenzo Sawyer issues an order making it illegal to dump tailings into the Sacramento and San Joaquin Rivers and their tributaries. This ruling essentially ends hydraulic mining.**

1895   The cyanide process of extracting gold from crushed ore is introduced at the mines of Bodie, California just beyond the eastern border of Yosemite near Mono Lake. This makes it possible to recover 95% of the gold from ore.

1898   **The first successful steam powered bucket-line dredge is used on the Feather River near Oroville. Gold dredging becomes a major gold producing industry.**

1922   The Argonaut Mine Disaster. A fire on the 3350 foot level of the Argonaut Mine near Jackson takes 47 lives.

1933   **The price of gold increases from $21 to $35 per ounce. This results in more exploration and greater production of gold in the state.**

Continued...

1942	World War II causes a drop in gold production. Congress issues Order L-208 on October 8. This forces the closure of all gold mining operations that use explosives and iron—materials critical for weapons production.
1946	**Order L-208 is lifted July 1. Some dredging resumes, but only a few important large-scale hardrock mines such as the Empire and North-Star in Grass Valley reopen.**
1957	The Empire and North-Star Mines in Grass Valley close down for good. Rising costs and the low price of gold collapse this most productive enterprise.
1965	**Governor Edmund Brown signs Bill 265 making gold California's official mineral. Thus the name *"Golden State."***
1968	The last gold dredge working near Oroville shuts down October 1.
1992	**The Columbus-America Discovery Group begins recovery of over 21 tons of gold that went down with the steamship *Central America*.**

Self-Test: Important Dates for California Gold

Copy the blank time line guide below on a separate piece of paper and organize the events for questions 1 through 8 in the order they happened. Expand your time line if you choose by adding extra entries from *Important Dates for California Gold* and from the *Gold Rush Era Time Line* on page 1.

1. By what year had the Gold Rush ended? _____

2. In 1898, what type of mining becomes a major industry?_____

3. What did Order L-208 do? _____

    _____

4. Why was the cyanide process important? _____

5. What was official when Governor Brown signed Bill 265? _____

6. How many men died in the Argonaut disaster of 1922? _____

7. Why were some Gold Rush towns ready for electrical generators when they became available?

    _____

    _____

8. What did the Columbus-American Discovery Group recover in 1992? _____

    _____

Y
e
a
r

E
v
e
n
t

Time saving hint: When writing answers to questions that do not have the year stated, write the year in your answer so you don't have to look it up twice.

VALUE OF GOLD IN THE 20TH CENTURY

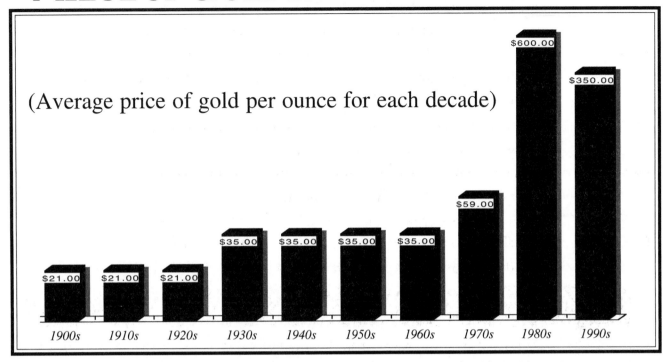

(Average price of gold per ounce for each decade)

$21.00	$21.00	$21.00	$35.00	$35.00	$35.00	$35.00	$59.00	$600.00	$350.00
1900s	1910s	1920s	1930s	1940s	1950s	1960s	1970s	1980s	1990s

Self-Test: Value of Gold in the 20th Century

Examine the average price of gold for each decade and answer the following:

1. What decade was gold worth the most? _____

2. Which decades did the price remain the most consistent? _____through_____

3. Find the difference in values between the highest and lowest decades: _____

4. What would be the *worst* decade to buy gold in order to make profit? _____

5. Find the average price of gold for all decades:_____ (Hint: total averages for all ten decades then divide by 10)

6. What is the current price of gold?* _____

   *(The current price of gold can be found in newspapers, TV or internet business news and coin shops)

   a. Is the answer to number five higher or lower than the current price? _____

   b. What is the difference? _____ c. What do you think causes this difference?

_____

_____

_____

WORK SPACE

Glossary of Terms

ARTIFACTS: Any object made or shaped by humans.

ALKALI(ZED): Natural concentrations of salt and mineral oxides that makes water bitter tasting. Drinking this kind of water can cause poisoning resulting in illness or even death.

AMALGAM: Combination of gold and mercury locked together that can only be separated with heat or acid.

ARGONAUT: An adventurer traveling by land or by sea.

ASSAYER: Person who is qualified to test the purity of minerals and determines their value.

BUFFALO CHIPS: Dried buffalo manure that can be used for fuel when wood is not available.

CHOLERA: An intestinal disease caused by bacteria that spreads quickly through infected food, water or bodily fluids and can be extremely deadly.

COMPANY: Groups of emigrants who agreed in a businesslike way to share the costs and responsibilities of travel.

CONTINENTAL DIVIDE: A mountain barrier such as the Rockies that divides Atlantic and Pacific bound rivers.

CYANIDE PROCESS: Method of extracting gold developed by German chemists. Powder fine crushed ore is added to a mixture of water and the poisonous chemical cyanide (that liquefies gold). This is then combined with zinc shavings (to capture the dissolved solution) and later separated. This process makes possible a 95% recovery of gold.

EMIGRANT: Person who travels from one location in a country to another.

ETHNIC GROUP: Race of people linked by a common language, beliefs, foods and artifacts.

FLUME: A sloping trough usually made of wood used to conveniently transport water over long distances.

FOUNDRY: A business that creates metal objects from molds such as parts for machines.

HARDROCK MINING: Type of mining where gold-rich quartz veins are picked and blasted apart. This creates deep mine shafts or open pits as miners follow the ore into the earth. The ore brought to the surface must then be crushed to extract the mineral.

HEADFRAME: Wood or iron support frame erected over the top of a mine shaft to which an engine connected to cables lowered and raised miners, equipment and ore carts on a track deep in the earth.

IRRIGATION: A method of artificially watering crops when natural rain is not present.

ISTHMUS: Narrow strip of land connecting two larger masses. The country of Panama is an example of this kind of geographical feature bonding North and South America together.

MALARIA: Type of disease transmitted by mosquitoes in temperate regions of the world. The illness causes high fever and eventual death without treatment.

Continued...

MERCURY: A heavy, silver-colored liquid metal also called quicksilver. This metal bonds with copper, gold and other metallic minerals and is used to trap microscopic gold particles.

MONITOR: The end piece of a hydraulic mining pipeline where the water exits. This final segment compressed the force of the water into a narrow diameter of anywhere from four to eight inches. This gave the water a powerful punch that could be directed at gold-bearing hillsides in order to wash material into a long sluice where the gold particles would be captured. Monitors were also known as "giants."

MOTHER LODE: California's rich gold region in the Sierran foothills from about Mariposa to Downieville. Although no single source or "lode" of gold existed as once thought, the name refers to the area where a majority of mineral wealth has been found.

ORE: Rock containing gold or other minerals that may or may not be easily seen within the rock.

PLACER GOLD: Loose, free gold that has been eroded from its original source.

PROSPECTOR: Person looking for a place gold is likely to be found.

QUARTZ: Generally a white-colored, glassy rock where many gold deposits originally formed. Most gold-bearing quartz veins are hidden underground, but parts of many reach the surface and are known as "outcroppings."

RAMMED EARTH: A Chinese method of constructing walls for buildings by mixing together a combination of clay, sand and limestone with very little water. The prepared mixture is packed inside a temporary hollow wooden frame six to nine feet in length and two or three feet wide which shaped a section. The contents are then pounded with metal rods from the top until the material is solidly compacted. The wooden frame is then removed. The end result provides a highly durable structure with superior insulation.

RETORT: Heating device used to separate gold from mercury once bonded together in a mining process.

SCURVY: Disease caused by a lack of vitamin C which is chiefly obtained from fresh fruits and vegetables. Symptoms of the illness include swelling of the gums, bleeding under the skin and general weakness resulting in death unless treated.

SLICKENS: Muddy combination of earth, rock and gold particles associated with hydraulic mining.

SLURRY: Runny mixture of water, powderized rock, and gold related to the operation of a stamp mill.

TAILINGS: Waste rock and/or mud remaining from various mining techniques used to extract gold.

TAILRACE: A "U" shaped open ditch diverted from a river used to control the flow of water that would turn a water wheel. After it turned the wheel creating power, the water continued through the ditch channel and returned to the river.

TECHNOLOGY: Inventions created to make life easier.

TRANSCONTINENTAL: To travel across or connect the length of a continent, as in highways, railroads or electronic communications.

VIGILANTE JUSTICE: A group or committee of citizens who administer justice in an emergency situation and immediately judge and punish an individual suspected of a crime.

Self-Test Answer Key Directory:

Self-Test Name:	Test Page:	Key Page:

Why Gold, Gold, Gold!......3......94

Background Summary......5......95

California Geography......8......96

The First People of California......11......97

Who Were the Goldseekers?......13......98

Transportation to the West......19......99

Voyage by Sea......25......100

Voyage by Sea to California (Map Activity)......26......101

Journey by Land......35......102

Journey by Land to California (Map Activity)...36......103

Where Gold is Found......37......104

Mining Methods......52......105

Mining Methods Crossword Puzzle......53......106

Pony Express......56......107

Telegraph (Morse Code Message)......58......108

Merced to Bear Valley......63......109

Hornitos to Sonora......67......110

Columbia to Stockton......72, 73......111-112

Mokelumne Hill to Fiddletown......77......113

Placerville to Nevada City......82, 83......114-115

Malakoff Diggings to Downieville......86, 87......116-117

Important Dates for California Gold......89......118

Value of Gold in the 20th Century......90......119

Self-Test Answer Keys

Why GOLD, GOLD, GOLD!

1. List three ways gold is used: *Special candy companies decorate chocolate with it, people wear it as jewelry, and it is used as a worldwide monetary exchange.*

2. How is gold important to our society? *Since it is valued in our society, it is used to back up our paper currency. It is also an incredibly versatile element that can be shaped into any imaginable form, and many regard it as a symbol of wealth.*

3. Why do you think gold is valuable? *Answers will vary...*

4. Provide at least one example of how California gold helped the growth of the United States: *Gold made more money available for loans which promoted economic development. Transportation routes such as railroads were also built with California gold.*

5. Describe one positive impact you think the goldseekers would have on Native Americans in California: *Answers will vary depending on background knowledge: The use of land would change with respect to farming by producing large surplus crops that would enable more people to pursue non-agricultural occupations; technology would also change the lives of the natives by improving transportation and communication methods making more opportunities available.*

Notes:

Self-Test: BACKGROUND SUMMARY

1. Name four early civilizations who used gold before Europeans explored the Americas:
The Egyptians, Greeks, Aztecs and Incas were using gold long before the Europeans crossed the oceans to explore the Americas.

2. Why didn't the Native Americans in California start their own rush for gold?
Gold was not important to their way of life nor was it a symbol of wealth in their society.

3. What European explorer made contact with California natives? Why did he stop here?
Did he learn anything about gold? *Sir Francis Drake was the English explorer who made contact with natives in California near present day San Francisco. He stopped here to make repairs on his ship, but never learned about California's gold.*

4. How might U. S. history be different if the Spanish had discovered gold first?
The Spanish may have colonized the west coast much more rapidly and held onto it. And with the arrival of thousands of their settlers, they might have expanded east which could have changed the course of United States history.

5. Who was Francisco Lopez? *He was a Mexican ranch hand near Los Angeles who was one of the first to realize a gold strike in California.*

6. What was the Bear Flag Revolt? *It was California's self-imposed government by Americans who were unhappy with Mexico's neglect. Helped by John C. Frémont's U. S. mapping expedition, the small army took Mexican California shortly before war officially broke out between the two countries.*

7. How was gold discovered in 1848 setting the Gold Rush in motion?
A carpenter named James Marshall found gold while constructing a saw mill on the south fork of the American River. The news would soon trigger a major rush to California.

8. Why did it take more than a year for the rush to begin? *Communications and roads to the far west were poor, and most people were not willing to risk a long, difficult journey into a relatively unknown part of the continent on hearsay. The President's 1848 speech and a gold display in Washington D. C. put doubts to rest and set the California Gold Rush in motion during the spring of 1849.*

CALIFORNIA GEOGRAPHY: *Self-Test*

This Self-Test will help you check what you have learned. Identify every feature from memory *before* writing Self-Test answers. Record symbols, letters, and numbers not remembered on the lines in the "restudy" box. If you need to review, examine study guide maps "A" and "B" again.

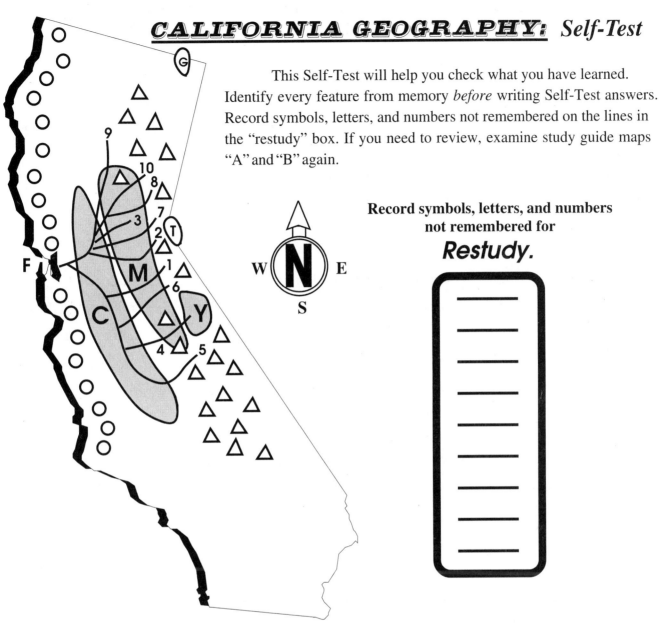

Record symbols, letters, and numbers not remembered for

Restudy.

LABEL THE FOLLOWING GEOGRAPHICAL FEATURES OF CALIFORNIA

(River numbers on Self-Test are different from map "B")

Rivers

1. *Stanislaus*
2. *Mokelumne*
3. *Bear*
4. *Merced*
5. *San Joaquin*
6. *Tuolumne*
7. *American*
8. *Yuba*
9. *Sacramento*
10. *Feather*

Lakes/Bay

G *Goose Lake*
T *Lake Tahoe*
F *San Francisco Bay*

Mountains

⟋◯⟍ *Sierra Nevada*
▢◯ *Coast Range*

Regions

M *Mother Lode*
Y *Yosemite*
S *Great Central Valley*

96

1. Describe Ahwahnee: *It is a beautiful valley shaped by the natural force of a glacier long ago. When the ice melted, rock walls and waterfalls thousands of feet high remained. Meadows, wildlife and food sources abounded in the protective environment of the valley we know as Yosemite today.*

2. Who were the Ahwahneechee and how did they become known as the Yosemites? *They were a group of Native Americans made up of various tribes. Collectively they were known as the Ahwahneechee since they lived in the valley they called Ahwahnee. It was a probable mispronunciation of the Indian word "Uzumaiti" which means "grizzly bear" that likely led to the miners knowing the Ahwahneechee as "Yosemites."*

3. What caused conflicts between the natives and miners? *Both cultures had different ideas of land use and property rights which led to conflict. A lack of understanding and fear often caused miners and Indians to react violently. For example, an Indian might see a miner's horse as an easy food target. And a miner might see the land he was searching for gold on as free for the taking.*

4. How did the Mariposa Battalion find the valley of Ahwahnee? *The Mariposa Battalion was organized to protect the interests of settlers by relocating the local natives onto a reservation. Led by James Savage, they were guided to the upper rim of the canyon in search of Tenaya and his tribe. It was here they first set eyes on Ahwahnee. Upon descending, the unmatched beauty of what we know as Yosemite Valley was revealed to them.*

Notes:

Self-Test: *WHO WERE THE GOLDSEEKERS?*

1. Where did the goldseekers come from? *They came from all walks of life and were overwhelmingly male. A majority of goldseekers were citizens of the United States, but ethnic groups from many regions around the globe were attracted as well.*

2. Define ethnic group: *A race of people united by a common language, beliefs, foods and artifacts.*

3. Why wasn't the journey to the gold fields what many expected? *Most hoped to make a fortune in California and return home in a year or two. But the reality was that they endured a long, difficult and deadly journey and when they got to California, few ever got rich.*

4. What influence did women have when they came west to California? *They had a civilizing affect on the men when they arrived. Women helped create a more stable family environment where homes and schools began to take hold.*

5. Imagine you are a young man or woman preparing to set out for California in 1849. Write a short letter explaining your reasons for going west to those you are leaving behind.

Dear _____,

Letters will vary but might revolve around gaining wealth and or seeing the west.

_____

_____

_____

_____

_____

_____

_____

_____

_____

Sincerely, _____

Self-Test: *TRANSPORTATION TO THE WEST*

Write a short description for each of the following methods of transportation. Include at least one advantage or disadvantage of each:

CONESTOGA WAGON

Large, heavy and well-built, these were excellent wagons. High ground clearance made traveling over washouts and tree stumps easier to pass. The upward slanting front and rear ends of the body kept belongings from falling out while going up or down steep hills. Their expense, size, and heavy loads they could carry, however, made them less popular and impractical for animals to pull on steep, mountainous roads during a long journey to California.

STANDARD WAGON

Smaller and less expensive than the Conestoga, this practical wagon was the choice for thousands of goldseekers. These boxy wagons were 12 to 14 feet long and covered with a canvas top that was often coated with a mixture of beeswax and linseed oil that served as a waterproofing. Outfitted with mule or ox teams of generally four to six animals, a wagon could comfortably haul 2000 pounds of provisions that would supply about five to California.

STEAMSHIP

Supplies that could not have been transported any other way to California in the early days of the Gold Rush were delivered by steamship. Powered by boilers producing steam that turned large side-mounted paddle wheels, these sturdy ships ranged from 100 to almost 300 feet in length. Most were also equipped with sails to take advantage of the wind or head-off the possibility of running out of fuel. Passengers had basic comforts, but keeping occupied during long uneventful days on the ocean was a disadvantage of this mode of travel. Although a voyage by sea could take as long as traveling by wagon, it was considered safer.

STAGECOACH

This was the fastest way west by land in the 1860s. A trip from St. Joseph to Sacramento averaged about three weeks. Stage travel was much more comfortable than a wagon because of a suspension system made of leather straps that ran under the coach's wooden body. 12 passengers plus two drivers could be seated in and on top of the coach. Cramped quarters and dusty conditions were the main discomforts of stage travel.

RAILROAD

Railroads had been operating in the U.S. since the 1830s, but it wasn't until 1869 that the transcontinental railroad connected the Atlantic and Pacific coasts of the United States. At an average speed of 20 miles per hour, it was a transportation breakthrough for the day. Even though making nearly 200 stops for water, fuel and passengers along the way, coast to coast travel now took less than a week.

Self-Test: VOYAGE BY SEA

1. Why didn't early newspaper reports convince most people in the eastern states there was really gold in California? *There was the possibility that reported stories of abundant gold might all be rumors, and people wanted to be sure. Also the expense and risk of the journey deterred potential goldseekers at first as well.*

2. What two things led people to believe there truly was a gold rush? *President Polk's 1848 State of the Union Address, and 230 ounces of gold displayed in the War Department convinced people.*

3. What were two advantages of the sea route compared to traveling by land? *It was generally considered safer than by land, and it could be faster if all went well on the shortest available route by way of Panama.*

4. Why wasn't the route through Panama always the best choice in 1849? *Disease such as malaria could be contracted. Also, in 1849 there was a good chance that a connecting ship on Panama's western shore would not be immediately available causing an extended wait.*

5. Why did many travelers choose the longer route around Cape Horn? *It was the surest way to guarantee passage to California without delay. Supply ships offered this voyage that lasted about 6 months.*

6. What were some of the problems aboard ship during the voyage? *Seasickness, fights, boredom and the fear one's ship could strike an obstacle in blinding fog or be torn up in a storm or all contributed to the problems during a voyage by sea.*

7. How did some captains deal with their situations when their crews abandoned ship in San Francisco? *They became business men by cutting up sections of their worn sails for tents, or renting their abandoned ships as warehouses, hotels, saloons etc... since construction could not keep up with the growth of this famous port city.*

8. What do you think is meant by: *Merchants were the ones who discovered the real gold mines.* *It can be inferred that merchants were all but guaranteed profits from the high-priced supplies they controlled and sold in their stores to the goldseekers who flooded San Francisco. Merchants "mined the miners" so to speak. It was also not as difficult to make a fortune when people brought it to you!*

MAPACTIVITY: *VOYAGE BY SEA TO CALIFORNIA*

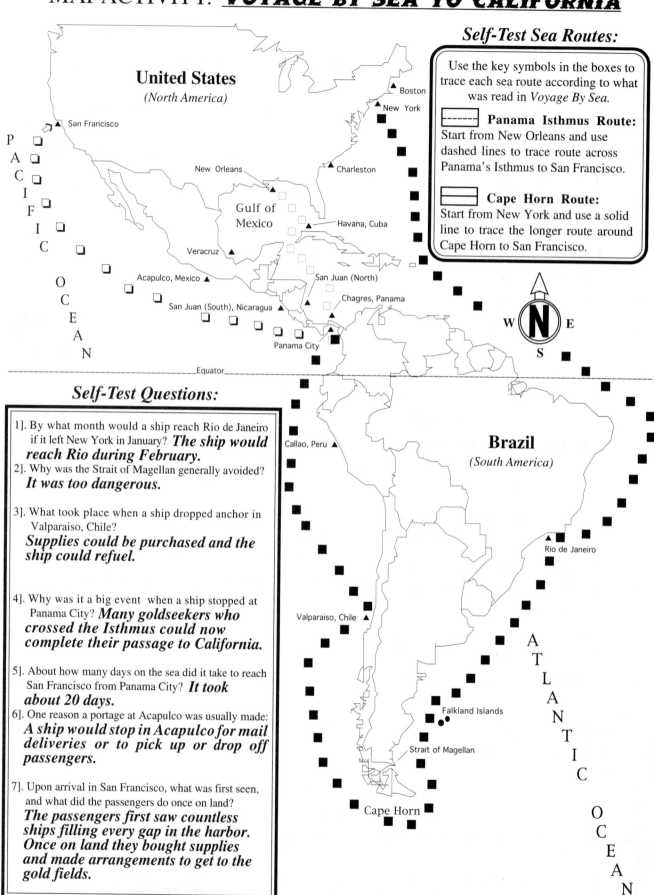

United States
(North America)

San Francisco

P
A
C
I
F
I
C

O
C
E
A
N

New Orleans

Gulf of
Mexico

Veracruz

Acapulco, Mexico ▲

San Juan (South), Nicaragua ▲

Panama City

Boston ▲

New York ▲

Charleston ▲

Havana, Cuba ▲

San Juan (North) ▲

Chagres, Panama ▲

Equator

Self-Test Sea Routes:

Use the key symbols in the boxes to
trace each sea route according to what
was read in *Voyage By Sea.*

Panama Isthmus Route:
Start from New Orleans and use
dashed lines to trace route across
Panama's Isthmus to San Francisco.

Cape Horn Route:
Start from New York and use a solid
line to trace the longer route around
Cape Horn to San Francisco.

W ⊕ N E
S

Callao, Peru ▲

Brazil
(South America)

Rio de Janeiro ▲

Valparaiso, Chile ▲

Falkland Islands

Strait of Magellan

Cape Horn

A
T
L
A
N
T
I
C

O
C
E
A
N

Self-Test Questions:

1]. By what month would a ship reach Rio de Janeiro
if it left New York in January? ***The ship would
reach Rio during February.***

2]. Why was the Strait of Magellan generally avoided?
It was too dangerous.

3]. What took place when a ship dropped anchor in
Valparaiso, Chile?
***Supplies could be purchased and the
ship could refuel.***

4]. Why was it a big event when a ship stopped at
Panama City? ***Many goldseekers who
crossed the Isthmus could now
complete their passage to California.***

5]. About how many days on the sea did it take to reach
San Francisco from Panama City? ***It took
about 20 days.***

6]. One reason a portage at Acapulco was usually made:
***A ship would stop in Acapulco for mail
deliveries or to pick up or drop off
passengers.***

7]. Upon arrival in San Francisco, what was first seen,
and what did the passengers do once on land?
***The passengers first saw countless
ships filling every gap in the harbor.
Once on land they bought supplies
and made arrangements to get to the
gold fields.***

Self-Test: JOURNEY BY LAND

A. An adventurer who traveled to California: A R G O N A U T

B. Groups of organized wagon train members called themselves a: _Company_

C. Month the journey usually began because grasses were tall enough for animals to graze: _May_

D. Two major cities where the trail west departed: _Independence_ and _St. Joseph_

E. Name the first river crossed at the start of the route: _Missouri_

F. Reason why the Oregon-California or Emigrants' Trail was popularly used: _It was the fastest most direct land route to the gold fields for most '49ers._

G. Animals generally chosen to pull wagons: _Mules or Oxen_

H. Name for continuous grasslands on first leg of trip: _Prairie_

I. Used for cooking fuel when there was no wood: _Buffalo chips_

J. Feared by the emigrants even though they caused little trouble: _Indians_

K. Major river flowing through Nebraska and Wyoming territories: _Platte River_

L. Name any two natural landmarks that were passed: _Courthouse, Chimney, Independence, Steeple Rocks, Scotts Bluff_

M. One reason military outposts were welcomed sights: _Buy supplies, mail letters, make repairs, rest_

N. Two diseases that killed or weakened many travelers: _Cholera and Scurvy_

O. Mountains entered through South Pass during the month of July: _Rockies_

P. Three reasons wagon animals died: _Bad or not enough water, malnutrition or exhaustion_

Q. Why some emigrants went to Salt Lake City, Utah: _To get supplies or rest_

R. Purpose wagons made a circle at night: _To keep their animals from running off or being stolen_

S. Caused Humboldt River water to become nearly undrinkable: _Alkali_

T. Average number of miles traveled each day by most goldseekers: _15_

U. Name of largest desert crossed in northwestern Nevada: _Black Rock Desert_

V. Name six foods eaten by pioneers: _Beans, bacon, flour, deer, buffalo, rice, dried apples etc..._

W. Other names given to the dangerous Lassen Cutoff: _"Green Horn" or "Death Route"_

X. Last mountains crossed to reach the California gold fields: _Sierra Nevada_

Y. Three reasons the final mountainous stretch was difficult: _It was steep, rocky and narrow. Snow could also be a factor in late fall too._

Z. Fort in modern day Sacramento where supplies could be purchased: _Sutter's Fort_

ACTIVITY: Write a personal diary for any three days of the six month adventure as if you were there in 1849 after rereading *Journey By Land*. Use your own paper and you can make it look "aged" by following the additional instructions below.

MAKE YOUR DIARY LOOKED AGED

A. Before you write, sponge very strong coffee or tea on your "diary pages."

B. While damp, tear off the outside page edges creating a "ragged" look, then using a candle in a safe place, singe the edges BEFORE the paper dries.

C. When dry, complete your diary using black or brown ink to add realism.

MAP ACTIVITY: *JOURNEY BY LAND TO CALIFORNIA*

The map below shows the 2000 mile **Emigrants' Trail via Lassen's Cutoff** from Missouri to Sutter's Fort, California. Do the following: **1).** Starting from St. Joseph or Independence, use a highlighter to *trace the route marked with <u>numbers and letters</u>* as described in *Journey By Land.* **2).** *Label Famous Landmarks "A through E"* in the box on the lines provided. Use the drawings below to match each landmark on the trail. **3). Complete the "Diary Box."** Imagine you are traveling to California in 1849. Start by choosing any one of the seven *region numbers*: they indicate various geographical locations along the trail such as prairie, mountains, deserts or plains. Also be sure to *record the approximate month* you would have been at your location. Then, *briefly describe one observation* such as your health, a campsite, weather or landmark referred to in *Journey By Land.* **4).** Finally, *label each outlined state*; use an atlas if needed.

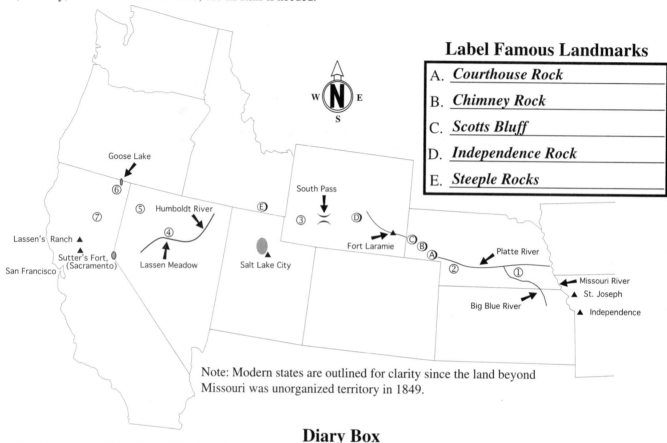

Label Famous Landmarks

A. *Courthouse Rock*

B. *Chimney Rock*

C. *Scotts Bluff*

D. *Independence Rock*

E. *Steeple Rocks*

Note: Modern states are outlined for clarity since the land beyond Missouri was unorganized territory in 1849.

Diary Box

*Region Number Choice:*_____ *Location:*_____ *Month:*_____,1849

Dear Diary, **Answers will vary, but each description should coordinate with a specific geographical region number and approximate month according to the text in *Journey By Land*. Location numbers / months are...**
1: prairie along the Big Blue / Platte Rivers (May/June);
2: sage-covered plain along the Platte River (June/July);
3: Rocky Mountains (July/August);
4: elevated desert basin along the Humboldt River (August/September);
5: Black Rock Desert (August/September);
6: uplifted plain in California (September/October);
7: Sierra Nevada Mountains (October/November).
*The writer must also include at least one observation appropriate to his/her selection based on events read in *Journey By Land*. The route should also be highlighted, famous landmarks labeled and outlined states named.*

F A M O U S   L A N D M A R K   D R A W I N G S

Courthouse Rock   **Chimney Rock**   **Scotts Bluff**   **Independence Rock**   **Steeple Rocks**

SACRAMENTO

The original site of Sutter's Fort (correctly pronounced *"Soot-er"*) turned out to be the perfect central location during the rush for gold. Combine that with overwhelming growth and influence, it became California's state capital in 1854. Like other Great Central Valley towns, Sacramento earned its importance as a supply and transportation hub. Situated where the American and Sacramento Rivers join, steamships could navigate all the way from San Francisco. And it wasn't too long before the railroad began conducting its share of material, people, and wealth fueled by the Gold Rush.

Sacramento in 1850. Prone to flooding, it was the main supply hub in the northern mines.
California State Library Archive

Spring floods often caused problems, but the city was always rebuilt and levees raised higher because of its prime position. It was a major starting point and wintering place for the first waves of goldseekers who came west. Businesses of all kinds were booming, and streets were flowing with overpriced goods and entertainment. Try to visit Old Sacramento City in the near future—it's loaded with unmatched historic sites and museums.

GRASS VALLEY & NEVADA CITY

Gold, timber, and grassland for livestock lured the first settlers to this area in 1848. Like many other settlements, Grass Valley might have faded into obscurity when its resources were exhausted, but it would not meet that fate. In 1850 the most productive, gold-laden quartz veins in the state were discovered in this vicinity and the town thrived for over a century because of it.

Hardrock mining was the leading method of gold extraction in the Grass Valley region, and it was developed with the help of Cornish miners from southern England who were experienced in blasting deep tunnels and shafts. But following quartz veins that run underground thousands of feet into the earth is not only dangerous, it is expensive, and large sums of money for equipment is required.

Investors from as far away as London bought in to this profitable venture. The two most important mines being the Empire and North-Star where stamp mills operated almost continuously from 1850 until 1957. This was California's richest area. At its peak eighty stamps milled ore 24 hours a day which eventually yielded about $400 million during that span of time. Presently, the two mines are excellent museums well worth making an effort to see.

Just a few miles north of Grass Valley is the town of Nevada City. Its hilly, narrow streets reminds one that geography was not an issue for city planning during the Gold Rush, and the town preserves that rustic attraction. It is also near the site where hydraulic mining was invented by a miner who used a small hand-sewn canvas hose to make his labor easier. His creation was soon further developed into huge iron water cannons that introduced yet another unique facet of mining history in the Golden State.

WHERE GOLD IS FOUND ✦

Notes: _____

_____
_____
_____
_____
_____
_____
_____
_____
_____
_____
_____
_____
_____
_____
_____
_____
_____
_____
_____
_____
_____
_____
_____

High Water Line

Beneath Sand Bars

Cracks in Rock

Between Rocks

Trapped in Grass Roots or Moss

Quartz Outcroppings

S T R E A M

♣ — Self-Test — ♣

After reading *Where Gold Is Found* and examining the drawing, list the six places it can be located then answer questions A and B.

1. *Beneath sand bars*
2. *Quartz outcroppings*
3. *Between rocks*
4. *Grass roots or moss*
5. *High water line*
6. *Cracks in rocks*

A. Why won't gold nuggets ever be found on top of sand? *Gold is heavier than the sand or gravel it lies in; therefore, gravity causes it to sink to the lowest point.*

B. A gallon container of water weighs 8 pounds, how much would the same container of gold weigh? (Hint multiply) *19 X 8 = 152 pounds*

104

Self-Test: MINING METHODS

A. Name the six methods miners used to recover *placer* gold:

1. _Panning_   4. _Long Tom_
2. _Cradle or Rocker_   5. _Sluice Box_
3. _Dredging_   6. _Hydraulic_

B. Name three *hardrock* mining devices that crushed quartz ore:

1. _Stamp Mill_   2. _Arrastra_   3. _Chilean Wheel_

C. Describe how a retort separates amalgam: _A glob of bonded gold and mercury is placed in the heating chamber. Then the metals are heated to molten temperatures. Since mercury vaporizes at a lower temperature than gold, it was the first to move through a cooling chamber. There it returned to its original form and was captured in a bucket to be used again. The gold left behind in the heating chamber, resembling a sponge when cooled, was the reward for all of the miner's time consuming work._

D. Write the name of the mining *instrument* that fits these words below:

1. GANTRY: _Dredge_   5. APRON: _Rocker_
2. MONITOR: _Hydraulic_   6. SPUD: _Dredge_
3. FLUME: _Sluice Box_   7. SLURRY: _Stamp Mill_
4. RIDDLE: _Long Tom_   8. SLICKENS: _Hydraulic_

E. Name one of the methods you read about and explain how cooperation between miners could improve their rewards: _(Example the rocker): If two miners cooperated using this method one could operate the rocker while the other collected buckets of gold-bearing sands and gravels keeping the process in motion. This would be less tiresome than working alone, and much more material could be sifted through in a day which would hopefully increase their profits if they worked very hard or were very lucky!_

F. Explain which mining technology was the most destructive to the environment:
Possible answer: Hydraulic mining because of the huge pits that rendered the land useless for any other purpose after the monitors had stopped. Additionally, the muddy waste tailings were generally dumped into a river system which filled the riverbed with silt destroying wildlife, impairing river boat travel and causing major flooding in the populated valleys below.

Mining Methods Crossword PUZZLE

ACROSS or BACKWARDS

1. Each crusher weighed 1000 pounds.

5. Another name for mercury.

6. Used a series of riffle bars to trap gold.

7. This machine left behind large piles of rock called "tailings."

8. The most basic way miners collected gold.

10. This method forced water through a "monitor."

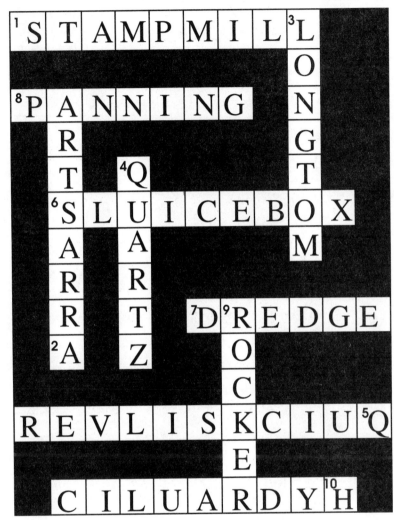

UP or DOWN

2. A mule pulled a flat stone to crush the gold ore.

3. Gravels were channeled down a trough before they ran over the "riddle."

4. Type of rock containing gold that was crushed by a Chilean wheel.

9. Also called a cradle.

106

SELF-TEST: PONY EXPRESS

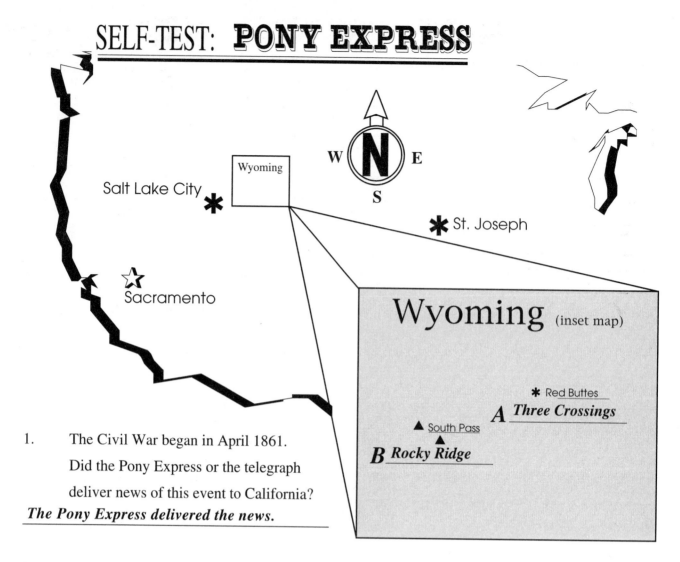

Wyoming (inset map)

* Red Buttes
A *Three Crossings*
▲ South Pass
B *Rocky Ridge*
▲

1. The Civil War began in April 1861. Did the Pony Express or the telegraph deliver news of this event to California? *The Pony Express delivered the news.*

2. On the inset map of Wyoming, label missing relay stations on lines **A** and **B** that were part of William Cody's famous 322 mile ride.

3. Why do you think the Express chose a route through Salt Lake City? *Possible answer: Salt Lake City was a populated area and many letters and desired news would go through there.*

4. How did the many relay stations receive supplies in their far off locations? *Supply wagons provided the necessary materials to support all the stations.*

5. What two factors contributed to the Pony Express going out of business? *Failure to ever make a profit and the transcontinental telegraph both caused the fall of the Pony Express.*

6. The actual Pony Express route was 1,890 miles long. If each rider rode 65 miles a day, how many had to be on duty? *29* (Hint: divide) How many miles would need to be covered in 24 hours to deliver the mail in 10 days? *189* (Hint: divide)

MORSE CODE KEY

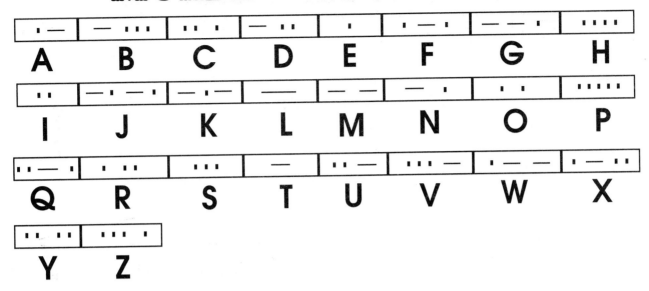

A	B	C	D	E	F	G	H
I	J	K	L	M	N	O	P
Q	R	S	T	U	V	W	X
Y	Z

**(Decode Judge Field's Transcontinental Telegraph Message On The Lines Below) **

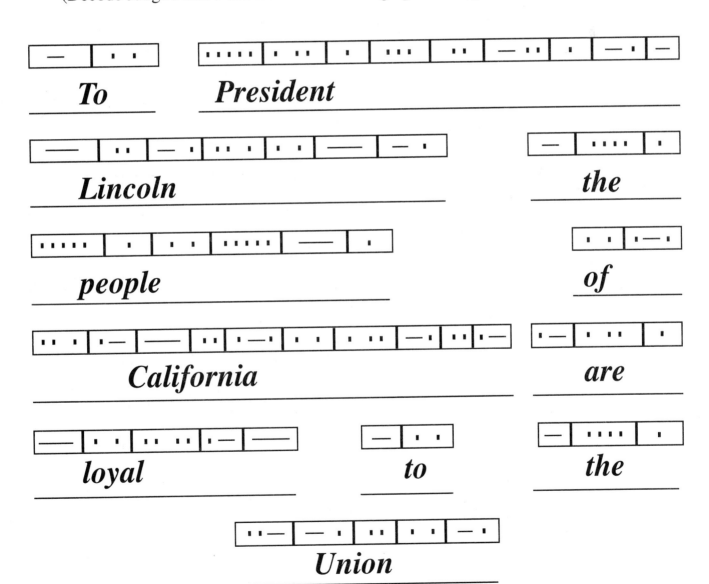

To President

Lincoln the

people of

California are

loyal to the

Union

Self-Test: MERCED TO BEAR VALLEY

1.   Describe the San Joaquin Valley before it was altered: *It was a beautiful semiarid basin with expansive grasslands, wetlands and rivers cutting through it. A variety of wildlife lived in this natural refuge. John Muir, a famous naturalist, as well as others commented that wild flowers abounded in the spring, but within two months everything turns brown. Today irrigation agriculture dominates the valley.*

2.   What was Snelling like before its decline? *It was a booming supply town with thousands of people. It contained Merced County's first courthouse, several hotels, and a variety of thriving businesses and services. The town declined over the years, but remains today as a small community.*

3.   Name three types of mills that operated in Merced Falls: *Flour, woolen and saw mills once churned out goods in Merced Falls.*

    a.   What kind of disaster destroyed the town in 1895? *Fire nearly ruined the town.*
    b.   Why did Merced Falls lose its importance? *A shortage of trees for the saw mill, the fading Yosemite Railroad and dredging restrictions soon collapsed the economy of the town.*

4.   Name the type of mining that took place at Mount Bullion: *Hardrock mining took place.*

5.   What town never produced $50 gold coins? *Mount Ophir never produced gold coins.*

    a. Why was the rumor started? *The legend that gold coins were minted in Mount Ophir was kept alive to increase tourism in the area.*

    b. What happened as a result of this rumor? *Would-be treasure hunters have destroyed the remaining buildings of this ghost town while searching for nonexistent gold.*

6.   Describe how large Mariposa County was at one time: *It was the largest county in California at one time. It extended to the Nevada border to the east, to the Great Central Valley to the west, near Los Angeles to the south and within reach of San Francisco in the north.*

7.   Briefly tell about John C. Frémont's life on his land grant: *Frémont had 44,386 acres purchased for him when Mexico still controlled California. When gold was discovered after the war with Mexico, he floated the unestablished boundaries of Las Mariposas to encompass the rich mines in the area. He was Bear Valley's most famous citizen as he was known for his military explorations, politics, and mining operation. Unfortunately he incurred huge expenses over the years and sold his land grant to pay debts.*

Self-Test: *HORNITOS TO SONORA*

1.   How did Hornitos get its name? *Probably from the oven-like burial mounds built by the Mexicans who lived there.*

    a.   What made Ghirardelli famous in San Francisco? *He became famous making chocolate.*

    b.   At its peak, how much gold was taken a month from Hornitos? *Thousands of dollars in rough gold was taken from Hornitos every month.*

2.   Why was the penalty for stealing a horse often worse than killing another person? *Sometimes arguments between individuals resulting in death may have been justified. But stealing a person's horse took away their ability to make a living of which there was no excuse.*

3.   How did Bret Harte become famous? *Harte became famous writing stories about the Gold Rush.*

    a.   What was the "Grey Goose?" *A massive 3000 ton dredge that sits in ruins today.*

4.   Describe how the "Whistling Billy" got to Coulterville and its purpose: *The Whistling Billy was a steam engine purchased by the Merced Mining Company. Shipped around the Horn of South America from the east coast of the United States, it arrived in San Francisco in 1897. From there it was taken in pieces by mule train to the foothills of Coulterville. Its purpose was to haul gold ore from the mountainous mines to the crushing mills below.*

5.   Why were the Chinese persecuted? *Their culture was so different from all others, they could be easily singled out.*

    a.   What is a tong? *A secret Chinese society.*

6.   What was the purpose of the Foreign Miners' Tax? *It was a tax designed to encourage citizenship, and raise money for the state by making foreigners pay a fee in order to work their claims. The tax was originally set at $20 per month, but repealed and then established at $3 per month.*

    a.   Explain why you think the tax was fair or unfair: *Answers will vary from: Paying the fee was the cost for the privilege of searching for gold in a foreign land, to politically correct responses, and/or revisionist history.*

    b.   Why did Sonora remain an important town after the gold was gone? *Sonora was part of a transportation route to Stockton, and was a major supply link to other mining camps. Today tourists still come to visit Sonora because of its historical significance during a livelier time.*

Self-Test: COLUMBIA TO STOCKTON

1.   Briefly summarize Columbia's history from 1850 to the present: *In 1850 miners camped at this location found gold while panning. The area was soon discovered to be the course of an ancient stream bed that was loaded with gold. Before long, hardrock and hydraulic mining equipment was operating in the area and the town rapidly grew. It became one of California's largest towns where a variety of stores, saloons and services thrived. Eventually the gold gave out and Columbia became a ghost town. But in 1945 the state of California bought most of the old buildings that survived and created a "Living" State Historical Park which has become one of the most popular Mother Lode towns.*

     a.   Why were buildings made from brick with metal doors and window coverings? *After a devastating fire burned most of the wooden structures in 1854, the town was rebuilt with fire resistant brick with metal door and window coverings to minimize future destruction by fire. The metal doors and windows served as a security feature for valuable goods as well.*

     b.   Explain what had to be done before hydraulic mining could take place: *Since the few creeks that ran through the area dried up during the summer months, two water companies built a system of ditches and a 60 mile long flume to supply the water that powered the hydraulic machinery that blasted the gold fragments locked inside hills.*

     c.   By the 1870s how much gold had been taken from Columbia? *$87 million was taken.*

2.   Describe the largest single mass of gold ever taken during the Gold Rush: *This mass of gold was taken from Carson Hill and weighed 195 pounds. It was four feet long, two feet wide and five inches thick mixed in quartz.*

3.   Contrast hardrock mining in its early days to similar mines today: *Hardrock mining in its earlier days was done by miners chiseling high-grade ore in deep tunnels by hand. Then a short iron cart called a "skip" was filled with half a ton of the valuable rock. A mule pulled the cart out on iron tracks that led to the crushing mill. Tunnels are now all but gone as large-scale open pit mining has made it possible to remove entire mountains with machinery and dump trucks that can haul almost 100 tons at once. But most gold today is microscopic and massive quantities of ore must be chemically processed to profit.*

4.   Name two books Mark Twain (Samuel Clemens) wrote: *The Adventures of Tom Sawyer and Huckleberry Finn and The Celebrated Jumping Frog of Calaveras County are two of his books.*

Continued...

SUPPLIES PURCHASED IN ANGELS CAMP:

(Items and prices taken from actual 1850 account. Prices varied greatly due to availability of goods—Supply and demand)

TOOLS

1 cradle	$18.00
1 pan	2.00
1 dipper	1.25
1 bucket	1.00
2 picks	10.50
1 shovel	11.00

TOTAL $43.75

FOOD

25 lbs. flour	$5.00
9 lbs. pork	2.70
4 lbs. beef	1.20
1 jar pickles	8.00
1 pint molasses	.50
2 lbs. sugar	.60
Ground coffee	5.00
2 lbs. potatoes	.25

TOTAL $23.25

OTHER

1 pair boots	$10.00
2 shirts	5.00
Pants	8.25
2 blankets	10.00
Canvas tent	30.00
2 candles	.50
1 mule	65.00

TOTAL $128.75

5. Hardrock mining kept Angels Camp productive for decades. What is meant by hardrock mining? *Hardrock mining starts with ore which is rock and gold mixed together. Since the ore is generally found in quartz veins that go underground, tunnels are dug into the earth by miners following the ore. Valuable rocks brought to the surface are then crushed by machines and the gold is separated from the waste.*

    a. Why did miners sometimes have to pay high prices for the things they needed? *It all depended on supply and demand. If goods were in short supply, the prices went up. Miners just paid the higher prices because by leaving their claim they could miss their chance to strike it rich.*

6. Why did Wells Fargo and Company build a station in nearly every rich boomtown? *They profited from the services they offered transporting mail, freight, passengers and gold. The glut of raw gold in boomtowns, made it possible to buy low and sell high at a later date; therefore, it was in their interest to locate their stations wherever quantities of people and gold gathered.*

7. What else made Murphys a one of a kind town other than gold? *Murphys had a bowling alley at one time, and the Murphys Hotel, built in 1856, is still in use so visitors can still spend the night there!*

8. Why did many paths lead to Stockton? *Stockton was a major supply center for miners and merchants going to or leaving the gold fields. The San Joaquin River connected Stockton with San Francisco, and land routes to Sonora, east, and Fort Miller, south insured a consistent supply of goods in the southern mining district.*

Self-Test: MOKELUMNE HILL TO FIDDLETOWN

1. Name two large ethnic groups who settled in Mokelumne Hill: *The French and Chileans of South America were two of the largest ethnic groups who populated this area.*

    a. What was one reason fights took place? *Since claims were staked closely together, arguments over mining rights broke out.*

2. Why did miners give Volcano its name, and was it accurate? *It was named so because miners thought the location was a crater of an extinct volcano. But the name was not accurate as the place was really an eroded bend of an extinct riverbed.*

    a. How did residents exercise their minds as well as the gold fields challenged their bodies? *They started organizations such as a lending library, theater group and debating society that exercised the mind as much as the labor of searching for gold challenged the body.*

3. What was Jackson's original name, and why was it named this? *"Botillas" was the original name which means bottles. Pioneers once stopped here for water at this natural spring.*

    a. Name the two mines where $34 million was taken: *The Kennedy and Argonaut Mines were the two largest producers of gold.*

    b. Describe why the four Kennedy Wheels were built: *Poisonous chemicals were used to process gold ore, and groundwater contamination became a concern. By 1912 the government passed laws forcing mining companies to contain their toxic wastes. The Kennedy Wheels, completed in 1914, elevated hazardous tailings uphill 128 feet to a holding dam.*

4. Why do many of Sutter Creek's buildings remain? *They were built with brick and stone that reflects the wealth of the town's past.*

    a. Why was the Knight Foundry important to hardrock miners? *It produced many of the metal parts required for hardrock mines and machinery.*

5. What was the purpose of the headframe in Amador City's Keystone mine? *It was a metal support frame that lowered and raised miners and ore carts in or out of the mine shaft.*

6. Name three mining methods used in Fiddletown: *Panning, hydraulic and stamp mills were the mining methods used in Fiddletown.*

    a. Summarize how a rammed earth wall is made: *It was an idea brought over by the Chinese during the Gold Rush. These durable, highly insulating walls were made from clay, sand and limestone. Hollow wooden frames were filled with the mixture of material and pounded with rods until solidly compacted. The support frames were then removed exposing the finished wall. They were built in 6 to 9 feet sections and were 2 to 3 feet thick.*

Self-Test: PLACERVILLE TO NEVADA CITY

1.   Describe how all three of Placerville's names came about: *It was originally named Dry Diggings because the streams dried up in the summer. As the town quickly blossomed, law breakers became a problem, and the citizens got fed up with it. Since justice was harsh and immediate, often by hanging, the name Hangtown stuck. Over time, however, citizens wanted to make the town sound like a more inviting place to stop, and they adopted the current name Placerville which refers to the large amounts of placer gold found there.*

    a.   What destroyed the town in 1856? *A tremendous fire destroyed the town.*

    b.   Name all of the changes in communication and transportation this town has seen in its early history: *Stagecoaches were the first major transportation link that ran through Placerville when a suitable route through the Sierra was opened. The telegraph also connected this town with other California cities even before the Pony Express rode through in 1860. By 1869 the Transcontinental Railroad passed through insuring that Placerville would not fade from existence.*

2.   What country controlled California when John Sutter arrived? *Mexico controlled California.*

    a. Write a summary for John Sutter and his role in the California Gold Rush:
John Augustus Sutter entered California by way of Hawaii in 1839 convincing the Mexican government in Monterey that they should allow him to open a trading post. They agreed, and he chose a site where the American and Sacramento Rivers converge. With the help of Indian labor, he had an adobe walled trading post built that resembled a fort. His venture thrived and he needed lumber for his growing demands. He hired a carpenter by the name of James Marshall to build a saw mill on the south fork of the American River some 40 miles away. It was during the construction of the mill in early 1848 that gold was discovered by Marshall who brought his find to Sutter. Word got out almost immediately and this time news of gold would spark the best-known Gold Rush in the world. But gold did not make Sutter rich; he could not control the flood of people who invaded and took over his property, and ended up selling his fort in the fall of 1849. He eventually relocated to Pennsylvania, and tried to recover his perceived losses in California from Congress. He died in Washington D. C. while making that attempt. The year was 1880.

Continued...

b. Write a summary for James Marshall and his role in the Gold Rush:

James Wilson Marshall was hired to build a saw mill on the American River by John Sutter. He began construction in a valley named Coloma by local natives. While inspecting the tailrace on the morning of January 24th, 1848 he found small pieces of gold. Returning to Sutter's Fort with his find, word soon spread of the discovery. Unknown to Marshall at the time he would be credited as the messenger that triggered the world's most famous gold rush. Like Sutter, gold never made Marshall rich. He tried his luck in business and also failed. Eventually he ended up in a small town near Coloma named Kelsey. There he operated a small blacksmith and carpenter shop. He was a heavy drinker and would autograph "gold discovery" cards commemorating the date of his find for a few cents. He wasn't even sure of the date himself, but it was realized in a crudely written diary by a laborer who helped build the saw mill. He died in 1885 with no family and was encased in a wagon on ice for five days before he was finally buried. Several years later the California State Legislature set aside money to build a monument in his honor. It stands atop his grave overlooking his gold discovery site in Coloma.

c. Explain why you believe Marshall was or was not a famous person in your opinion:

Answers will vary: Some may consider him famous because he is credited with the discovery that set off California's Gold Rush. Others may not feel Marshall was as important possibly because he was not recognized during his lifetime as a hero. It wasn't until years later that a statue was built in his honor acknowledging his claim to fame, but one that failed to make him rich!

3. What crime had its beginnings in Auburn? *The first recorded stagecoach robbery took place here.*

4. Provide at least three reasons why Sacramento was an important city during the Gold Rush:
It was a major supply center and "jumping-off" point for goldseekers. It was linked to San Francisco via the Sacramento River. In 1854 it became California's state capitol because of its location and growth.

a. What natural disaster was a problem for Sacramento in its early days? *Flooding was a problem but the city was always rebuilt.*

5. Why did people first settle in Grass Valley? *Gold, timber and grasslands for livestock attracted the first settlers to Grass Valley.*

a. Name the two largest hardrock mines in the area and the total amount of gold taken from them: *The Empire and North-Star Mines operated from 1850 until 1957 where a total of $400 million was taken in all.*

6. What mining method was invented near Nevada City? *Hydraulic mining had its roots here.*

Self-Test: MALAKOFF DIGGINGS TO DOWNIEVILLE

1. Describe the hydraulic mining pit at Malakoff: *It is a huge crater 600 feet deep, a mile and a half long and half a mile wide. The bottom of the pit once had seven monitors that pounded the hillsides for the bits of gold they possessed.*

    a. How many pounds did the largest block of gold taken at Malakoff weigh? *It weighed 510 lbs.*

    b. How long were the shifts miners worked in this operation? *Miners worked continuous eight hour shifts around the clock.*

    c. How many gallons of water could the largest monitor discharge in one hour? *1 million gallons per hour could be discharged from the largest monitor.*

    d. What town was flooded as a result of hydraulic mining? *Marysville was flooded.*

    e. This town supplied the miners at Malakoff Diggings: *The town was North Bloomfield.*

2. Name the mining method that developed near Oroville: *Dredging was developed here.*

    a. Who was Ishi? *He was possibly the last "wild" California native in existence. When everything he had known was taken or destroyed; hunger and loneliness finally drove him from the mountains.*

3. What "first" is Downieville known for? *This town is known for hanging the first woman in California. She was found guilty by a vigilance committee for having murdered a miner.*

    a. Name the last town in the northern Sierra where the Mother Lode ends: *It is Sierraville.*

4. Interpret how California has progressed economically from the end of the Gold Rush until now: *When the rush for gold had ended those who remained in California realized the potential for wealth in other areas. Agriculture and the timber industry as well as tourism among many others would keep California's economy booming. It is California's wonderful climate and beautiful landscapes and resources that have shaped the state's future and continue to do so today.*

Continued...

5. Looking back on all of the towns you read about, describe the kinds of changes that took place in California during the Gold Rush era, and how they improved the quality of life:

Answers may include: Advances in communication: for example, mail to telegraph services; transportation: wagons to the speed of railroads; energy technologies: water power to electricity; developments in gold mining methods; the emerging importance of agriculture, timber and tourism in California; the transformation of the towns that started from tent camps and either survived the test of time or ended as a ghost town. Even the ruins of California's historical landscapes have an impact on us today making it possible to look back and reflect on the places that built the state. (Descriptions of any or all of these topics as well as others can be related as to how they improved the quality of life).

6. Why are historical Gold Rush towns worth preserving? *Possible answers might include: They provide a means so we can visit the past and know where we came from. They also help make us aware of the way technology has made our lives easier and has impacted our environment. The towns that still exist are our window into history. They help us understand the people of a time long ago and keep our own values and destinations in focus.*

Self-Test: Important Dates for California Gold

1. By what year had the Gold Rush ended? *It ended by 1854 because yearly production decreased.*

2. In 1898, what type of mining becomes a major industry? *Dredging becomes a major gold producer.*

3. What did Order L-208 do? *Congress forced all gold mining operations that used iron and explosives to stop because of WWII in 1942.*

4. Why was the cyanide process important? *In 1895 miners could recover 95% of the gold from ore.*

5. What was official when Governor Brown signed Bill 265? *California's state mineral was gold in 1965.*

6. How many men died in the Argonaut disaster of 1922? *47 men lost their lives in the Argonaut mine.*

7. Why were some Gold Rush towns ready for electrical generators when they became available? *The same water systems used for hydraulic operations and to irrigate fields provided a ready source of power for this inexpensive energy when electrical generators became available in 1880.*

8. What did the Columbus-American Discovery Group recover in 1992? *The Columbus-America Discovery Group began recovery of 21 tons of gold that sank with the SS Central America in 1857.*

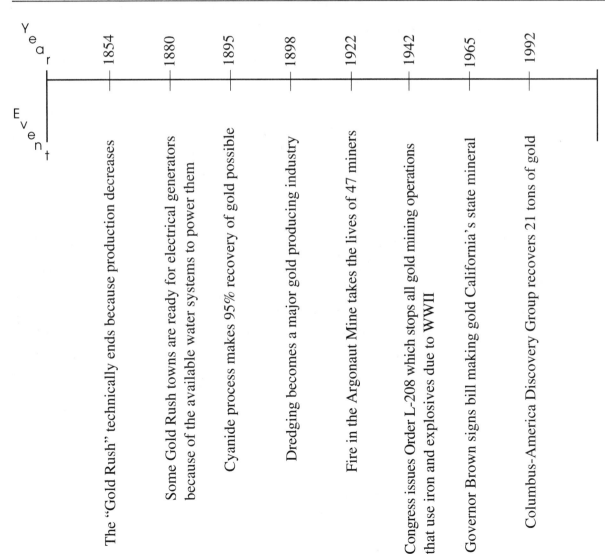

Year

| 1854 | 1880 | 1895 | 1898 | 1922 | 1942 | 1965 | 1992 |

Event

- The "Gold Rush" technically ends because production decreases
- Some Gold Rush towns are ready for electrical generators because of the available water systems to power them
- Cyanide process makes 95% recovery of gold possible
- Dredging becomes a major gold producing industry
- Fire in the Argonaut Mine takes the lives of 47 miners
- Congress issues Order L-208 which stops all gold mining operations that use iron and explosives due to WWII
- Governor Brown signs bill making gold California's state mineral
- Columbus-America Discovery Group recovers 21 tons of gold

VALUE OF GOLD IN THE 20TH CENTURY

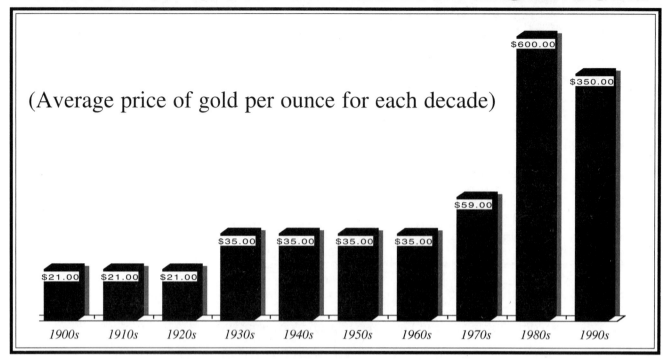

(Average price of gold per ounce for each decade)

| | | | | | | | | $600.00 | |
| | | | | | | | | | $350.00 |

$59.00

$35.00 $35.00 $35.00 $35.00

$21.00 $21.00 $21.00

1900s 1910s 1920s 1930s 1940s 1950s 1960s 1970s 1980s 1990s

Self-Test: Value of Gold in the 20th Century

Examine the average price of gold for each decade and answer the following:

1. What decade was gold worth the most? __*1980s*__

2. Which decades did the price remain the most consistent? __*1930s*__ through __*1960s*__

3. Find the difference in values between the highest and lowest decades: __*$579*__

4. What would be the *worst* decade to buy gold in order to make profit? __*1980s*__

5. Find the average price of gold for all decades: __*$121.20*__ (Hint: total averages for all ten decades then divide by 10)

6. What is the current price of gold?* _____

    *(The current price of gold can be found in newspapers, TV or internet business news and coin shops)

      a. Is the answer to number five higher or lower than the current price? __*Lower (As of 1/02)*__

      b. What is the difference? __*(Will vary)*__ c. What do you think causes this difference?

Possible answers may include: The scarcity of gold; The historical stability of gold generally stays
consistent for long periods of time and often does not fall below previous highs; Economic inflation
helps maintain a higher price of gold since, to some degree, it backs up the value of paper currency.

WORK SPACE

Bibliography *(Selected)*

Bancroft, Hubert Howe. *History of California*. 7 vols. San Francisco: 1890. California History Co., 1886—90.

Borthwick, J. D. *3 Years In California*. With a foreword by Joseph A. Sullivan. California: Biobooks, 1948.

Bruff, J. Goldsborough. *Gold Rush: The Journals, Drawings and other papers of J. Goldsborough Bruff... April 2, 1849—July 20, 1851*. 2 Vols. Edited by Georgia Willis and Ruth Gaines. New York: Columbia University Press, 1944.

Beck, Warren A. and Ynez D. Haase. *Historical Atlas of California*. Oklahoma: University of Oklahoma Press, 1974.

Cabezut-Ortiz, Delores J. *Merced County: The Golden Harvest*. Windsor Publications Inc., 1980.

California Department of Parks and Recreation. Sacramento. *Gold Dredge*. Publications Section, 1993.

California Historical Society. *California Gold Discovery: Centennial Papers on the Time, Site and Artifacts*. San Francisco: California Historical Society, Reprinted from California Historical Society Quarterly Vol. XXVI, No. 2, 1947.

Cooke, Alistair. *Alistair Cooke's America*. New York: Alfred A. Knopf Inc., 1973.

Frémont, John Charles. *The Expeditions of John Charles Frémont*. 3 Vols. Edited by Donald Jackson and Mary Lee Spence. Chicago: University of Illinois Press. 1970, 1973, 1984.

Gay, Theressa. *James W. Marshall the Discoverer of Gold in California*. Georgetown, California: The Talisman Press, 1967.

Gudde, Erwin G. *California Gold Camps: A Geographical and Historical Dictionary of Camps, Towns, and Localities Where Gold Was Found and Mined: Wayside Stations and Trading Centers*. Berkeley: University of California Press, 1975.

Hammond, George P. *The Weber Era in Stockton History*. Berkeley: University of California Press, 1982.

Hanna, Warren L. *Lost Harbor*. Berkeley: University of California Press, 1979.

Holliday, J. S. *The World Rushed In*. New York: Simon and Schuster, 1981.

Johnston, Hank. *Railroads of the Yosemite Valley*. California: Interurban Press, Reprint, 1963.

Kemble, John Haskell. *The Panama Route, 1848—1869*. University of California Publications in History, Vol. 29. Columbia: University of South Carolina Press, Reprint 1990.

Kraus, George. *High Road to Promontory: Building the Central Pacific across the High Sierra*. Palo Alto, California: American West Publishing Company, 1969.

Kroeber, Theodora. *Ishi In Two Worlds: A Biography of the Last Wild Indian in North America*. Berkeley: University of California Press, 1961.

Lewis, Oscar. *Sea Routes to the Gold Fields*. New York: Alfred A. Knopf, Inc., 1949.

May, Phillip Ross. *Origins of Hydraulic Mining in California*. Oakland, California: The Holmes Book Co., 1970.

Morgan, Dale L. *The Humboldt: Highroad of the West*. Freeport, New York: Books for Libraries Press, Reprint, 1971.

Paul, Rodman W. *The California Gold Discovery: Sources, Documents, Accounts and Memoirs Relating to the Discovery of Gold at Sutter's Mill*. Georgetown, California: The Talisman Press, 1966.

Perkins, William. *Three Years in California: William Perkins' Journal of Life at Sonora, 1849—1852*. With an Introduction and annotation by Dale L. Morgan and James R. Scobie. Berkeley: University of California Press, 1964.

Russell, Carl Parcher. *One Hundred Years in Yosemite*. Berkeley: University of California Press, Reprint, 1947.

Schatz, Barry and Judy Conrad editors. *Story Of An American Tragedy: Survivor's Accounts of the Sinking of the Steamship Central America*. Ohio: Columbus-America Discovery Group Inc., 1988.

Settle, Raymond W. and Mary Lund Settle. *Saddles and Spurs*. Harrisburg, Pennsylvania, 1955.

Vronski and Westerman. "*History of Gold*." Gold Digest. N. pag. Online. Internet. 1997-2001. Available http://www.gold-eagle.com/gold_digest/history_gold.html

Wagner, Jack R. *Gold Mines of California*. San Diego, California: Howell-North Books, 1980.

Ware, Joseph E. *The Emigrants' Guide to California*. Reprinted from 1849 edition with an introduction and notes by John Caughey. Princeton, New Jersey, 1932.

Zollinger, James Peter. *Sutter: The Man and His Empire*. New York: Oxford University Press, 1939.

Index

A

Acapulco, Mexico 24
Ahwahneechee, Indians 9, 10, 11
Amador City 76
Amalgam 50
American River 4, 21, 79, 81
Angels Camp 70
Argonaut 22, 23, 24, 27, 91
Argonaut Mine 75
   disaster 88
Arrastra 47
Assayer 39, 70
Auburn 80

B

Bear Flag Republic 4
Big Blue River *28*, 36
Black Rock Desert 31
Bodie, California 88

C

Cape Horn 23, 65
Carson City 57
Carson Hill 69
Carson River 31
Central America, SS (lost gold)
   1, 22, 88
Central American crossings 24
Central Pacific Railroad 1, 61, 78, 80
Chabot, Antoine 42
Chagres, Panama 22
Chew Kee Store 76
Chilean wheel 48
Chimney Rock 29, 36
Chinese 18, 65, 66
   construction of stone fences 59
   rammed earth building construction
   76, 92
Chinese Camp 66
Cholera 29, 30
Churches 12, 24, 30, 68, 78
Civil War 1, 2, 18, 56, 69
Clemens, Samuel 69. *See* Mark Twain
Clipper ship 21, 23
Coast Range 7, 24
Coloma 79, 80
Columbus-America Discovery Group
   22, 89
Continental Divide 30
Cornish miners 81
Cost of travel 16, 22

Courthouse Rock, Nebraska 29, 36
Cutoffs 30, 31
Cyanide process 75, 88, 91

D

Discovery of gold 79
Disease 29, 34
Donner Party
   *reference to 30
Drake, Sir Francis
   explorer in California 4
Dredging 1
   explained 44
Dry Diggings 78

E

Electric power 1, 43, 44, 88
Emigrants' Trail 27, 36, 103
Empire Mine 1, 89
   museum 81
Entertainment 23, 68
"Eureka" 85

F

Falkland Islands 23
Feather River 43, 44, 85
Fiddletown 76
Foods 23, 27
   Hangtown Fry 78
Foreign Miners' Tax 66
Fort
   Bridger 30
   Kearney 57
   Laramie 29
   Miller 71
Forty-Niner ('49er) 20, 27, 31, 37
Frémont, John C. 4, 24, 31, 62
French 65, 74

G

Geography of California 6, 7
Giant 42. *See also* monitor or water
   cannon
Gold
   value of 1, 88, 90
   where found 37
Gold discovery 79
Golden Gate
   *named by Frémont 24
Golden State 2, 12, 44, 81, 85
   defined 89
Goose Lake 7, 34
Grass Valley 81
Great Central Valley
   6, 10, 24, 34, 43, 46, 61, 81

H

Hangtown 78
Hardrock mining
   38, 47, 48, 49, 70, 76, 81
Highway 49: 37, 59, 60, 65
Hornitos 64
Humboldt River 31
Hydraulic mining 1, 42, 68, 74, 84

I

Important Gold Rush Dates 1, 88, 89
Independence, Missouri 27
Independence Rock, Wyoming 29, 36
Indians 2, 9, 10, 11, 55, 71, 79, 85
Irrigation 6, 43, 61
Ishi 85
Isthmus of Panama 14, 22, 24, 26

J

Jackson 75
Jails 24, 62

K

Kelsey 80
Kennedy Mine
   Wheels 75
Keystone Mine 76
Knight Foundry 75

L

La Grange 65
Lassen's Cutoff 31
Lassen's Ranch 34
Long tom 41
Lopez, Francisco 4, 5, 88

M

Malakoff Diggings 60, 84
Malaria 23
Maps of California 6, 7, 8, 96
Maps:
   Gold Rush Towns 60
   Journey by Land 36
   Pony Express 56
   Transcontinental Railroad 18
   Transcontinental Telegraph 57
   Voyage by Sea 26
Mariposa 62
   Battalion 10
Marshall, James 79
   statue of 80
Marysville 24, 44
Mattison, Edward 42
Merced 61

Merced Falls 61
Merced Mining Company 65
Merced River 9, 10, 61
Mercury 46, 47, 48, 50, 51, 92
Mexico 1, 4, 24, 27, 62, 66
Mine shafts 69, 70, 75, 76, 91
Mining Methods 38-50, 88
Missouri River 28
Miwok, Indians 10
Moffat, John L. 62
Mokelumne Hill 74
Monitor 43, 76, 84
Mormons 30, 80
Morse Code 57, 58
Mother Lode 6, 12, 59, 62, 92
Mount Bullion 62
Mount Ophir 62
Muir, John 61
Murphys 71

N

Native Americans 4, 9. *See also*
    Indians
Nevada City 81
New Helvetia 79
New York 23
Nicaragua 16, 24, 26
North Bloomfield 84
North-Star Mine 1, 81, 89
    museum 81

O

Open pit mining 43, 69
Ore 38, 47, 70, 75, 92. *See* Hardrock
    mining
Oregon-California Trail 27
Oroville 44, 88, 89

P

Paiute, Indians 55
Panama 16
    City 23
    Isthmus Route 22
Panning 39
Phoenix
    first use of dredge 44
Placer gold 38, 78
Placer gold (mining) 39-46, 92
Placerville 78
Platte River 29
Polk, James K. 21
Pony Express 1, 54, 57, 78
Promontory Summit, Utah 18

Q

Quartz 37, 70, 88. *See also* Ore
Quicksilver 48, 50, 51, 92. *See also*
    Mercury

R

Rabbit Hole Wells 32
Railroad 1, 2, 14, 18, 61, 78
Rammed earth structure 76
Retort 51, 92
Rio de Janiero 23
Rivers of California 7
Rocker
    also known as "cradle" 40
Rocky Mountains 29, 30, 55
Russell, William 54

S

Sacramento 1, 18, 24, 81
Sacramento River 24, 81, 84
Salt Lake City, Utah 30, 55, 57
San Francisco 22, 24, 43, 64, 71, 81
    Bay 7, 14, 24, 84
San Joaquin River 24, 71
San Joaquin Valley 6, 61, 71, 85
Savage, James 10
Sawyer, Lorenzo 43, 88
Scotts Bluff, Nebraska 15, 29, 36
Scurvy 34
Ships 16, 23
Sickness 9, 23. *See also* Disease
Sierra 78, 85
Sierra Nevada 7, 9, 18, 33, 34, 61
Sierraville 85
Slickens 42
Sluice box 41
Sonora 66
Sources of gold 37
South America 14, 23, 41, 48, 65, 74
    map of 26
St. Joseph, Missouri 17, 27, 54
Stagecoach 17, 24, 54, 71, 78, 80
Stamp mill 49, 62, 76
Steamships 14, 16, 81
Steeple Rocks, Idaho 30, 36
Stockton 24, 66, 71
Strait of Magellan 23
Sublett's Cutoff 30
Sutter Creek 75
Sutter, John 79
    Fort 34, 54, 81
    Mill 1, 79, 80
Sweetwater River 30

T

Tahoe, Lake 7, 31, 78
Tailings 46, 50, 84, 92
Telegraph 55. *See* Transcontinental
Tenaya, Chief 10
Time line 1, 88
Tong War 66
Trans-Sierran 78
Transcontinental
    Railroad 18
        *first in North America 14. *See
        also* Railroad
    Telegraph 57
Truckee River 31
Tunnels 69, 70, 75, 76. *See also* Mine
    shafts
Twain, Mark 54, 69, 70

U

Union Pacific Railroad 18
United States
    1, 2, 4, 12, 14, 18, 21, 41, 66
Utah 18. *See* Salt Lake City
Utica Mine 70
Uzumaiti 10

V

Valparaiso, Chile 23
Veracruz, Mexico 24
Vigilante justice 78, 85
Volcano 74

W

Wagons
    descriptions of 15
War with Mexico 1, 21, 62
Ware, Joseph E.
    *mention of guidebook 28
Washington D. C. 1, 21
Water cannon 38, 43, 81
Water power 43, 61, 68
Wells Fargo 64, 65, 68, 70, 71
Where gold is found 37
Whistling Billy 65
World War II 1, 46, 89

Y

Yosemite
    name of 11
    Railroad 61
    Valley 9, 61
Yuba River 44, 84, 85

A Guide to the California Gold Rush
By Eugene R. Hart

 Please photocopy or hand copy the information on this page to place an order.

Order Form

Name or Organization: _____

Address: _____

State: _____   Zip: _____

Please send _____ book(s) at $24.50 each. Total $_____

Price <u>includes</u> tax, shipping and handling!

Do not send cash. Send check or money order for prompt delivery to:

> FreeWheel Publications
> 1173 El Portal Drive
> Merced, CA 95340-0676

Thank you for your order!

Printed in the United States of America

© 1993, 2002